ENDORSEMENT FOR *BEFORE I GO*

We live in a society which practically worships youth, anti-aging and physical fitness. Therefore the draw to older individuals whose face and steps might show signs of aging is out-of-favor in our worldly culture. I beg us all to remember God's design from the beginning—we all need each other! Young and old, we all need each other. No talented, young preacher who is full of godly living can give us advice on 50 years of ministry. This book is a rare opportunity to go to the city gates to listen to the wisdom of our elders. This book is our modern-day likeness of Paul sharing with Timothy. This book is an abundant resource flowing from some of the godliest, friendliest, wisest, and most humble servants who have walked the same path of ministry we have walked, but for longer. Read the wisdom that comes from their godly hearts after decades of heralding trips to the pulpit and countless hours of service with the towel. Let's glean from hearts that have been shaped through perseverance and minds which have been renewed more Mondays than we might imagine.

What a gift! To each of you half-century or longer preachers, we deeply, with great gratitude, thank you for your life's example and this book.

To each younger reader, let's enjoy and learn from the wisdom of these tenured servants. Now, our cup runs over.
David Shannon, Mt. Juliet, TN

The Jenkins Institute delivers another treasure trove of practical and helpful advice from some of the most respected teachers, preachers and leaders in the church today. It has been my privilege over the years to have quality association with the great men who have contributed to this book. Each of them has excelled in their particular areas of ministry and has added great value to the lives of multitudes of people. Young preachers, do yourselves a favor and take advantage of the wealth of wisdom offered in this historic work. The stories, illustrations and antidotes are priceless and the solid Biblical principles taught will serve as a formula for success throughout your lives. I give Before I Go my highest recommendation.
Dennis Jones, Heritage Christian University, Florence, AL

One of the warmest epistles of the NT is Paul's second letter to Timothy. An older brother and fellow preacher wrote—via the inspiration of God—to encourage a younger preacher. If we were searching for words to entitle this book of the Bible, we might call it, "Before I Go." Paul wanted Timothy to reignite a flame for preaching (2 Tim. 1:3-7) and remember some things before his departure (2 Tim. 4:6). Along that same line of thought, the volume you are now holding offers sage counsel from fourteen wonderful

brothers in Jesus. Read it carefully, digest its advise methodically and enjoy the path of service yet in your future. God bless,
Dan Winkler, Huntingdon, TN

It's amazing to me how the apostle Paul started many of his letters. In at least nine of the letters, Paul started with the attitude of gratitude. For example, to the Romans he writes, "First, I thank my God through Jesus Christ for all of you..." (1:8). Like Paul, I am thankful for my brethren--especially my preaching brethren. We are who we are because of the people who have preceded us. We all stand on the shoulders of those who have gone before us. One of the reasons that I am a preacher today is because of the love, wisdom, encouragement, and example of older preachers. This book is about preaching and is written by seasoned and experienced preachers. Listen to their counsel. Learn from their wisdom. Lean on their example. Live their messages. Love their Lord. This book will make a difference in your life and will help you continue to make a difference in the lives of others.
Keith Parker, Hendersonville, TN

It was about fifteen years ago when it dawned on me that I was already older than the preachers who had tremendously influenced me when I was a teenager and a college student. That realization, painful though it was, is what caused my wife and me to begin a mentoring group for young couples who were heading into full-time church ministry. I still remembered how hungry I was at their age to know what really went on behind the scenes in the lives of my preaching heroes. As I developed the curriculum for that group, I focused on the hard-to-teach-in-a-classroom lessons that I had come to know were the make-or-break issues in a minister's life. The outline for our mentoring group looked a lot like the table of contents of Before I Go.

I believe this book will be a wonderful gift to all young ministers. While I've certainly known the work of all these writers, I have only known half of them personally. The ones I know have always demonstrated a keen interest in helping the younger generation of preachers in whatever way they can. They have earned our respect and the right to be heard. And, if I might use one of my favorite expressions, they have all demonstrated the power of "a long obedience in the same direction." Every minister should heed the call of Paul for us to "pass on" the faith to the next generation of leaders. This allows us to have a hand in preaching the gospel to generations we will never see. An expression of this wise divine plan is seen in Before I Go. I enthusiastically recommend both these men and their essays to the next generation of preachers.
Bruce McLarty, Harding University, Searcy, AR

BEFORE I GO

Notes from Older Preachers

presented by
The Jenkins Institute

ISBN-13: 978-1517026486
ISBN-10: 1517026482

Published by The Jenkins Institute

thejenkinsinstitute.com

Cover design: Josh Feit, Evangela.com
Interior layout: Joey Sparks
Professional editing: Kathy Jarrell

One of our dad's favorite quotes was: "The future is as bright as the promises of God." That sort of optimistic outlook endeared Jerry A. Jenkins to many. The picture on the front of this book is of dad and his grandsons. It was taken in front of the N.B. Hardeman Library in Memphis. All of these young men have preached some. It is with that same optimism and hope for the future that we dedicate this volume to young preachers everywhere. They inspire us and help us to believe the future is indeed bright. They energize us and renew us. We pray and trust they will be men of the Word their whole lives.

May this book bless you as these contributors have blessed us.

ACKNOWLEDGEMENTS & THANKS

In *Men In Black-I,* Will Smith says to Tommy Lee Jones "you know what the difference is between you and me? I make this suit look good." In this work there are a lot of people who make us look a whole lot better than we are.

Of course when we start thinking of who makes us look good we'd have to start with the women who stand beside us. All you have to do it look at a picture of us then of Laura and Melanie and you can SEE that. But it goes much deeper than that. These two godly women model Christianity in front of us every day. They also patiently allow us to travel, speak, study and minister and support us in those endeavors. We are blessed.

The team that helps bring books for TJI from concept to reality take the words and projects we are a part of and help us produce the materials you have in your hands. Joey Sparks pays attention to the details and formatting of our books in ways that if it was left in our hands we'd throw them in the air and nothing we work on would ever get completed. Kathy Jarrell worked as format editor at Vanderbilt, then moved to Granny White and edited my (Dale's) drivel—it must have been like going from being an art critic at the Louvre to reading the Sunday comics. But I trust her pen—even though it be brutal! Josh Feit at Evangela can communicate through a cover a whole book. We're so thankful for the help of each of these professionals.

Obviously this book would not have a reason to exist were it not for the lives of the writers. They bring wisdom, humility, faith and faithfulness to the table—but most of all they bring lives lived in the service of the Lord. While we are thankful for their skills it's their lives that caused us to call upon them to share insights with others. So, may we say it this way: Thank you for living for the Lord.

We are both blessed to be a part of local ministry. It's really all we've ever known so we want to say thank you to those congregations and the elders who patiently struggle with the time we take away to strive to minister to other ministers.

Finally thank you! Yes, you. Without a reader what would a writer be? We believe God has great things in store for your life. You'll never regret investing it with Him and His Cause. May He always richly bless you.

CONTENTS

FORWARD

"...preach the word; be ready in season and out of season; reprove, rebuke, and exhort, with complete patience and teaching" (2 Timothy 4:2).

Of Epapharus: "He is Christ's faithful servant, and he is helping us" (Colossians 1:7).

" Now in a great house there are not only vessels of gold and silver but also of wood and clay, some for honorable use, some for dishonorable. Therefore, if anyone cleanses himself from what is dishonorable, he will be a vessel for honorable use, set apart as holy, useful to the master of the house, ready for every good work" (2 Timothy 2:20-21).

We love preachers and have been inspired by them to be better. Preaching and loving others who preach is in our blood—it is part of our DNA—it is why The Jenkins Institute was birthed. It honors the one who modeled loving preachers to us BUT more than that, the One who taught us what love is.

We want to be better preachers, but more than that to be better servants and stewards of God's goodness. Recently we were discussing how several powerful voices through the years are no longer around and how their influence is missing. What would those senior voices of experience say to a younger preacher today? How would they encourage you? How would they react to the current state of things?

So many of the voices of influence in the church have passed on and we find ourselves wishing they had left a direct word to younger guys. Frankly we wish someone had done something like this a long time ago, but the best time to begin a journey is today. We've asked these heroes to write as if they were sitting down across from a young preacher and just talking. We thank them and we know you will be blessed. Within this group there are over 1,000 combined years of Gospel Preaching—over 100,000 lessons preached—these men have said much and still have much to say.

The Jenkins Institute
Jeff and Dale Jenkins

1

THE HEART OF PRECHING

Jay Lockhart

Since I was a teenager I knew I wanted to give my life to preaching the gospel. After college, I began fulltime preaching in 1961 and have been involved in local work for fifty-four years. During more than half a century I have had many experiences and, hopefully, have learned some lessons which can be helpful to younger preachers. Having reached my seventy-seventh year, I am committed to continuing my work of preaching for as long as the Lord permits. However, I realize that the time will come when I will be unable to do this work. Therefore, "before I go" I want to write down some suggestions about preaching which I hope will be remembered by those who preach the glorious message of the everlasting gospel both now and in the future.

1. Remember that an effective preacher must preach because he must. From a human point of view Jeremiah was one of the most unsuccessful preachers in history. For forty years, he spoke the word of God to a rebellious people, not many of whom wanted to hear the message. He was laughed at, ridiculed, beaten, put in stocks, imprisoned, thrown into a partially dry cistern, and threatened with death. He became so discouraged that he wanted to quit. He said, "I will not make mention of Him, nor speak any more in His name," (Jeremiah 20:9—all Scripture quotations will be from the NKJV unless otherwise noted). However, Jeremiah could not refrain from speaking for God and he cried, "But His word was in my heart like a burning fire shut up in my bones; I was weary of holding it back, but I could not." Those who preach the gospel must do so because they have a fire in their bones and they preach because they have to.

2. Remember that nothing can take the place of study. The preacher's work involves so many opportunities including visitation, personal evangelism, writing, traveling among the churches, speaking engagements in various settings, funerals, weddings, and the need to spend time with his family. However, the preacher must remember that the preparation and delivery of effective sermons takes

time and is hard work. In preparing a sermon, the preacher deals with a text of Scripture. He must discover and understand the immediate context, as well as, the larger context of the book from which his text is taken. He must know who wrote the book (if possible), to whom it is addressed, and why it was written.

He must answer three questions about the text. First, what does it say? This question can be answered by carefully reading the text several times from various translations and in the original languages, if possible. Second, what does it mean? The answer to this question is only discovered by careful study and by asking other questions: What is the author's major theme and purpose in the text? What are the key words in the text? What do these words mean in the original languages? What is the author's purpose? How may the text be outlined? What is my purpose in preaching from this text? How may the text be illustrated? Third, how does it apply? The task of preaching is not completed until the message is applied to the life of the hearer.

To properly answer these questions the preacher must set aside large blocks of time for study each week. With the many demands made upon the preacher's time, it will sometimes be difficult to give as much time to study as needed. However, nothing can replace the careful preparation of sermons, and adequate time must be allocated for study. A preacher who continues to study can remain fresh in his presentations and can stay with one church for many years.

3. Remember that preaching must be undergirded with prayer. In studying the Bible one needs wisdom to properly understand and apply the Scriptures. James stated the principle, "If any of you lacks wisdom, let him ask of God,...and it will be given to him" (James 1:5). This certainly can be applied to any area of life in which we need wisdom, so let the preacher saturate his message with prayer. Let him pray as he studies the text. Let him pray for his comprehension. Let him pray for the people who will hear the message. Let him pray for clarity in his delivery of the message. Let him pray for the proper response to the message.

4. Remember what preaching is. John A. Broadus, who wrote and talked much about preaching, said that preaching is "proclamation through personality." The power in preaching is in the message, but the message cannot be separated from the "earthen vessels" (2 Cor. 4:7) who speak the message. However, the vessels must never get in the way of the message. So, what is preaching? The two basic words in the New Testament which demonstrate what preaching is are: (1) euaggelidzō, meaning "to bring good news" (Thayer 256); and (2) kērussō, meaning "to proclaim to persons one whom they are to become acquainted with in order to learn what they ought to do" (Thayer 346). Biblical preaching, then, becomes nothing short of an

encounter with God, as the preacher engages in the exposition of the word of God. Every preacher should recognize this truth.

5. Remember what the message of preaching is. Paul told Timothy to preach "the word" (2 Tim. 4:2). The Greek term translated "word" is logos and means in this context "the doctrine concerning the attainment through Christ of salvation in the kingdom of God (Thayer 381). Further, Paul reminded the elders of the church in Ephesus that he had declared to them "the whole counsel of God" (Acts 20:27). The words "the whole counsel of God" translate the Greek phrase "pasan tēn boulēn meaning "all...the totality" (pas: see Zodhiates 946 and Bullinger 38) of the "will...; purpose, design, plan" (boulē: see Bullinger 189) of God. Thus, Thayer gives the meaning as "all the contents of the divine plan" (Thayer 104-105). Here is the preacher's responsibility: to preach all of God's word. This is why the preacher is to be an expositor of God's message. He should preach through books in the Old and New Testaments. He should preach through chapters and paragraphs. His job is to expose all of God's will to the hearer. Until one understands what the message is, he cannot be a faithful proclaimer of it.

6. Remember that most people who hear you appreciate hearing biblical preaching. The people come where preaching takes place wanting to know, "Is there any word from the Lord?" (Jeremiah 37:17). The

preacher's task is to answer affirmatively that there is a word from God and then to declare it. When the preacher exposes that message by giving its meaning, illustrating its truth, and applying its principles, people will come to love the word of God.

7. Remember that biblical preaching is powerful to meet man's greatest needs. What are the greatest needs of human beings? The first great need is to be saved from sin, and the word of God meets this need. Paul declared that the gospel "is the power of God unto salvation" (Rom. 1:16). The gospel is powerful to transform sinners into saints and it needs to be preached in its fullness to all men. The second great need is to grow and mature as a Christian, to develop "into the image of Christ" (Rom. 8:29), and the message preached can fulfill this need. As Paul took his leave of the elders of the church in Ephesus he said, "So now, brethren, I commend you to God and to the word of His grace, which is able to build you up and give you an inheritance among those who are sanctified" (Acts 20:32). So, preach the word and never be surprised when people are transformed by it.

8. Remember that the preacher must be genuine. This means that he is to be honest, humble, and one who practices what he preaches. The preacher will be ineffective if the people who hear him have the impression that he is a hypocrite. This does not mean he is perfect, but it does mean that he is serious about living the new life in Christ, that he is quick to forgive,

and that he readily apologizes for his mista

9. Remember that the points of a sermo clearly presented and tied together. An ef sermon has an attention-getting introduct conclusion that summarizes the message a... response. Between these two important parts of a sermon the points must be carefully and plainly stated. I have heard sermons, and have probably preached more than my share, that were filled with good thoughts, but afterward I wondered what points the preacher was trying to make. If I want my sermons to be remembered and if I want them to change lives, I need to clearly and distinctly present the points and help the hearer know when I leave one point and go to the next.

10. Remember that you are the preacher for all the people. Of course the preacher will have some people in the congregation to whom he feels closer than he does to others, but he is the preacher for all. This means he will make an effort to treat all members alike and will not slight one in order to serve another to whom he feels closer. This is not easy to do, but it will make for a happier and more effective ministry and might even allow the preacher to stay at one place longer than he might otherwise have stayed. If the preacher will get to know people and become a part of their lives, he will be a more effective preacher.

11. Remember that some capable men have ruined their ministries by engaging in inappropriate

relationships with women. Whenever a married preacher gives un-due attention to a woman other than his wife or allows a woman, not his wife, to give un-due attention to him, trouble is ahead. If the preacher finds this happening to him, he must stop it at once. Otherwise, he will cause, sooner or later, untold heartache for himself, the other person involved, his family, and the church. The preacher must always be on his guard to avoid any kind of compromising moral situations. If the preacher visits in the home of a woman who is alone he should take someone with him. If a woman comes to his office he should leave the door ajar or have someone else nearby.

12. Remember to make the best use of your time. To my knowledge no one has ever questioned whether or not I am on the job. To prevent this I have always kept office hours. This does not mean I am always in the office. Some of the office time is used for the preparation of sermons and classes, some is used for writing, some is used for correspondence, and some is used for meeting with people. I visit hospitals, nursing homes, and in the homes of members (I usually take my wife or elder or another member with me for these visits). I do not spend much time with members who drop by my office with nothing to do. After a few minutes I find ways to conclude the visit. I do not spend a lot of time trying to win battles having to do with opinions. I try to choose my battles carefully because not everything is worth going to mat for.

Even if it is a matter of Scripture, I try to be gentle and kind in standing for the truth (see 2 Timothy 2:24-26). I spend time with my elders as we talk about various aspects of church life. Since we know each other well and respect one another's viewpoints, I have avoided any serious problems with the elders with whom I have worked over a period of more than fifty years. In making the best use of my time, I allocate time for my family. When my children were growing up, and now watching my grandchildren grow, I have tried to spend meaningful time with them. We vacation together; we go to their games and other school activities, and sometimes just "hang out" together. I remember the words of Song of Solomon 1:6: "They made me the keeper of the vineyard, but my own vineyard I have not kept." In trying to save others, I do not want to neglect my own family.

These are some of the things that should be remembered by those who preach. No doubt there are many other things that need to be remembered which are as important as these. However, these are things that have been helpful to others, and I am hopeful they will be beneficial to those who read these words as together we continue the work of preaching the gospel, motivated by the fact that there is "a fire burning in our bones" and we preach because we must.

REFERENCES

Bullinger, Ethelbert W., A Critical Lexicon and Concordance to the English and Greek New Testament. (London: Samuel Bagster and Sons, n.d.; reprint, Grand Rapids, MI: Zondervan Publishing), 1975.

Thayer, Henry, A Greek-English Lexicon of the New Testament (New York, NY: Harper and Brothers, 1889; reprint, Chicago, IL: American Book Company), n.d.

Zodhiates, Spiros, The Complete Word Study New Testament (Chattanoga, TN: AMB Publishers, 2nd Edition), 1992.

2

A HEART FOR PEOPLE

John Dale

While I don't consider myself a great role model for young preachers, I love preaching and I love preachers of all ages. My 51 years in the pulpit have led me to appreciate the blessings of God and of God's people. My prayer is that these words will be truthful and helpful to someone, perhaps more than one.

In an effort to form an environment for this writing, I've tried to envision myself sitting with my grandsons when they're in their mid-teens discussing their options for service in God's kingdom. They have asked me to give them insight and advice that can help to steer them in the right direction, and hopefully to avoid some of the pitfalls that can come with inexperience.

Growing older is an opportunity for wisdom and clarity. Moses admonished in Psalm 90:4,12:"For a thousand years in Your sight are like yesterday when it is past, and like a watch in the night...So teach us to number our days that we may gain a heart of wisdom." The apostle Paul referred to himself as one of Christ's older and bolder prisoners: "for love's sake I rather appeal to you; being such a one as Paul, the aged, and now also a prisoner of Jesus Christ."(Philemon 8-9). Jean-Paul Sartre said, "The more sand that has escaped from the hourglass of our life, the clearer we should see through it." Spending time with younger folks, especially young preachers, is one of the greatest tonics an older guy can find. We're not competitors, nor are we to resent the successes of one another. We're on the same team, just playing different positions. No army can be successful unless the soldiers work together toward the common goal of defeating the enemy and preserving, protecting and defending the peace. And no army should shoot its wounded.

Two conversations with my earthly father helped me form the basis for today's admonition to younger preachers. The first occurred when I was 17 years old. I let Dad know that I planned to enroll in Freed-Hardeman as a Bible major. He said, "If you choose to be a preacher, I'll be mighty proud of you, but I'd be equally proud of you if you choose some other profession just as long as you're faithful to God. I don't care what you do for a living just as long you're faithful to God." Then he said, "But if you are going to preach, stay out of the pulpit until you're sure you know the Golden Rule, and if you do know the Golden Rule, don't ever ridicule another person's faith." Today, I wish I could say I've always practiced what Dad taught. However, regardless of my flaws in this area, I've always known better than to make fun of others' beliefs. When I've practiced the Golden Rule in that setting, or any other for that matter, I've never looked back and been ashamed of having chosen that compassionate course of action.

The second memorable conversation with my Dad took place 10 years later, just a week before he passed from this life at age 61. Confident that he wouldn't live much longer, he wanted to talk with me about some paper work that would need attention. He closed by saying, "And I've spared you three boys a lot of headaches; there isn't any money for you to fuss over." I responded, "I don't think we'd fuss over it anyway, but praise God what you're leaving us cannot be bought with money." The memory and example of a Christian man who determined to be faithful no matter what life dealt him, to provide the best he could for his three sons, and to be totally committed to Christ and His church, are worth far more than all this world's goods combined. With the absence of his wife following the birth of their third son (I who speak unto you am he!), Dad had to make up his mind how to cope. He had only a high school education, so his financial opportunities were limited, but his incredible work ethic and confidence in God's providence would guide his family through whatever would come. He inspired my brothers and me to choose to interpret life's adversities in this way: Pray fervently for what you want and for what you think is best. Accept whatever comes as a means to spiritual growth. If the answer is good, thank and praise God who is the giver of every good and perfect gift (James 1:17). If what happens is not good, pray that God will work in it for good and to His ultimate glory (Rom. 8:28).

At age 19, facing the challenge of severe mistreatment by an authority figure, a brother in Christ, I had to decide how I would respond and react. The temptation was powerful to write off everyone as hypocritical and self-serving. To give up my hopes and dreams of being a preacher, replacing those worthy goals with cynicism and negativity seemed a real option, albeit a poor option. With inestimable help from my beloved preacher and mentor, B. B. James, I received advice which has sculpted my attitude and actions for a lifetime of dealing with people. His advice was, "Keep every human being at sufficient distance so as not to be allowed to destroy you. Trust God absolutely! Trust people properly, not improperly, and that includes brethren, leaders, friends, family, everyone!" While suspicion and paranoia, should be avoided, it's wise to remember that every human being is fallible and is capable of misunderstanding, of weakness and temptation; only God can be worshiped. You have only one Lord, Jesus Christ of Nazareth. Keep everyone else at some place after Him!

If I had a thousand lifetimes to live over, I would want to be a preacher every time. I'd also be sure to have additional academic preparation to be a "tent maker" if/when the need arose to support my family in ways other than preaching.

If I had a thousand lifetimes to live over, I would want to marry Marsha every time. I'd want the same two children and same two grandchildren. Be careful to treat your family with love and affirmation. It takes both quality and quantity time. It's worth the time and energy you'll expend. Failure to do so can complicate or even sabotage your effectiveness in dealing with people.

These accounts of my life and family are not intended to be "Woe is me!" stories to generate sympathy, nor should they be interpreted as boastful ("Look what we did!"). They are shared with the hope that they will provide encouragement to young men who are seriously considering ministry areas, especially those that will include staff positions in churches of Christ.

In my conversation with my grandsons, I would want to be sure to cover some areas of concern, caution, and encouragement. So in addition to Golden Rule treatment of others, keeping all human relationships at sufficient distance so as not to allow anyone to come between my Lord and me, and responding maturely to the curve balls life can throw at us, I would want to encourage them to accept personal responsibility for their own attitudes, actions, and words (Ezek. 18:20; 2 Cor. 5:10).

I would emphasize that honesty is not only the best policy, it is the only policy! Tell the truth every time; never cheat even in small things (Rom. 12:17; Eph. 4:25-32).

Rather than worry and fret, spend time in prayer with thanksgiving (Phil. 4:6; Matt. 6:19-34).

Place the best interpretation possible on what others say and do; give them the benefit of the doubt. The judging of hearts is in good hands, not yours and mine (Matt. 7:1-5; James 2:13).

Put your whole heart into whatever you do, and do it enthusiastically and with passion (Ecc. 9:10; Col. 3:23).

Develop a heart of genuine gratitude, and express praise and thanks continually (Psalm 100; Luke 17:11-19).

The unexamined faith is not worth having, so don't fear truth. Ask questions, and then ask more questions (Prov. 23:23; James 1:5).

Guard your influence (Matt. 5:13-16; 1 Tim. 4:12). Avoid evil and the appearance of evil (Rom. 12:9; 1 Thess. 5:22).

Be forgiving of those who have sinned and are penitent (Matt. 18:21-35).

Settle disagreements and differences while they are still small (Phil. 2:1-5; 4:2-3).

Learn the distinction between guilt and consequences. Guilt can be completely handled through Christ's blood and our relying on Him. Consequences may last a lifetime.

Make up your mind what is most important and worth fighting for. Emphasize the things that are worthy of your attention (cf. Matt. 6:33). Sometimes we express this concept by such expressions as 'You gotta pick your fights,' or 'I'll take a bullet for that,' and 'This ain't the hill I choose to die on.' For instance, I'll take a bullet over the resurrection of Christ, but I won't take a bullet over translations, orphans' homes, or types of songs.

Make moral choices that will honor the Lord whose name we wear. Don't play with fire expecting never to get burned. Ask 'What would Jesus do?' and 'What would Jesus have me do in my circumstances?' and 'What would I do if Jesus were literally walking beside me?'!

"Preach the gospel at all times, and when necessary use words." (Francis of Assisi, Charles F. Brannon, et. al.). Some people will remember what we say; most everyone will remember what we do and how we made them feel. Edgar A. Guest got it right when he wrote, "I'd rather see a sermon than hear one any day; I'd rather one would walk with me than merely tell the way...The best of all the preachers are the men who live their creeds; To see the good in action is what everybody needs."

These guideline and caution flags are worthy of your consideration, and mine, every day and under all circumstances.

Teach and influence by your words and your life. Help people learn and obey the gospel of Christ and live for Him who died for us. Look forward to the eternal rewards awaiting the faithful.

Rejoice in the Lord! Grow in the Lord! Someday, die in the Lord! Bless you, my brothers! I love you, and God loves you more!

3

BUILDING STRONG RELATIONSHIPS WITH ELDERS

Dan Jenkins

I owe a great debt to those older preachers who spent many hours with me as I began working at a congregation which had elders. I owe those preachers a tremendous debt and one way of repaying that debt is to share with younger preachers truths I learned from them. Because of the passing of time, 55 years to be exact, my experiences may not be identical to yours, but there are many principles which will help every preacher in every age.

A major factor in the success or failure of the work you do with any local congregation is the kind of relationship you have with the leadership in that church. From the beginning create and maintain the spirit of being part of a team with the eldership. Know their view of the church and share with them your dreams for what that congregation can become. Having a common goal helps ensure that your work with them will be pleasant. The words of Paul have been part of my heart in working with elders to describe our mutual goal—"that we may present every man perfect in Christ" (Col.1:28).

That "Tryout" Sermon

It all begins with a conversation or a phone call. First impressions are so important - you must be yourself, not just portraying an image you think might impress them. As things progress, there will be that invitation to visit the congregation. How you respond to the elders in these early conversations will set the stage for the relationship you will have for them as long as they know you. True enough, their behavior will have an impact on you. You have little control over what they do, but total control over your own actions.

My older brother, Jerry, gave me some advice before I first worked under any eldership. It has meant so much to me over the years. One sentence he said is as fresh in my memory as the day he said it. It seems to sum up what our behavior should be in beginning days of a relationship with a congregation. He said, "Dan, when you go to try out at a congregation, do not preach your best sermon." That sounded so strange when he said it, but I have learned to appreciate it even more over the years. If you preach your best sermon when you go, the church will expect you to equal that in every sermon you preach—and you never will! Obviously you would not preach you worst sermon, but do not ever present yourself as something you are not! If you take "best sermon" approach, the church will always be disappointed in your preaching. Likely the elders will begin to question their wisdom in asking you to become their preacher.

In your initial communication with elders talk openly about what you envision for that congregation, but be careful. You need time to learn the abilities of that church. Do not misunderstand what I am saying. You need to "sell yourself" to the eldership and the congregations, but make sure that the self you sell is who you really are and the goals you set are reasonable.

It is far better to arrive at a work and surprise people about your abilities than for them to be disappointed. So as those first impressions are being formed, just be yourself. Solomon said it this way, "Let another man praise you, and not your own mouth" (Pro. 27:2).

Starting the Work, Setting the Parameters

There is probably no period more important in developing the proper relationship with elders than those first few meetings you will have with your elders. It is imperative that everyone involved has a clear understanding of the expectations they have of each other. Obviously, the financial side is important. This involves many factors like salary, medical insurance, housing consideration (especially if the house is provided by the church and when and how matters concerning the house will be handled), vacations, number of weeks away for gospel meetings and lectureships, annual raises, remuneration for miles driven in serving the Lord and host of others things. There should be great clarity about these matters. If notes are not taken you might consider sending an email to the elders after the meeting just to avoid future conflict. Your future relationship with the elders should not be hampered by failure to clarify these matters at the beginning.

Then there are the expectations of the job descriptions for both elders and preachers. At this time when you relationship is at a high point, get them to describe what they see as your work and the expectations of how you will spend your time. It's likely they will assume you will be just like the other preachers they have had and will automatically think you will know your role. Those preachers may have functioned as the "errand boy" for the church, handling the details of every problem which needs to be fixed. If that is how they see your work, you need to know this. The former preachers may have spent most of their time visiting members, contacting the wayward, visiting every sick person in the hospital and being at the beck and call of every elder and deacon in the church, sometimes even at the beck and call of every member. Meeting all these expectations often gives you little time to do the true work of an evangelist.

You need to know the elders' view of how you should spend your time. Do they have an expectation of the hours you should spend in the office each day? Do they have an understanding of the amount of time you need to study for Bible classes, sermons and personal growth? Do they understand how you should fulfill His charge to you to "do the work of an evangelist?" Do they understand the importance of the time you must spend with your family? An older preacher said to me years ago, "If I save the whole world and my children are lost, I will have wasted my life." Just keep in mind there is no eldership that will totally share your answers to the matters mentioned above, but you should begin the work clearly understanding their expectations of you. The joy you will have in the years you are there can be enhanced by these early meetings.

Let them verbalize to you their view of their work. How have they dealt with wayward members in the past? Do the elders ever visit the wayward, or do they just let them drift away from the church? Has the church ever practiced church discipline and for what reason was it done? Dealing with these matters at the beginning is so important. When talking about this, do not have a haughty spirit as though you are conducting an inquisition but simply to learn how they will proceed when situations develop in the future.

There is also a need for a mutual understanding of the way problems facing the church should be handled. Where do the elders stand on the clear proclamation of the unique nature of the church, various aspects of worship, the role of women, marriage and divorce, modesty, social drinking and other matters which confront the church? Assure them of your balanced approach in these matters and your commitment to preach the truth in love You need to know they will "have your back."

Being a Cheerleader for the Elders

If you want to have the best relationship with the elders let them know they can be assured of your support. Then, by your actions let them develop the trust that you are their defender and that you will have their back. This concept is precisely what Paul told Timothy about how he should work with the elders at Ephesus. He told young Timothy to never receive an accusation against an elder except at the mouth of two or three witnesses. In this same context he told Timothy: "Let the elder who rules well be counted worthy of double honor" (1 Tim. 5:17). That is so easy to do when elders are faithfully doing their work.

The rub comes when there are elders who do not shepherd well. It will happen and there are some things you must prayerfully consider ahead of the time. When the time comes that you must deal with an elder who is not doing what you think he should do, how should you respond? I am not taking about sinful actions, but when he has lost sight of what he should be. At that time I urge you to read 1 Samuel chapters 24 and 26. King Saul was far from what he should have been, but David simply would not strike one who had been anointed by God. He said, "The Lord forbid that I should stretch out my hand against the Lord's anointed" (1 Sam. 26:11). As Saul was chosen by God, the Holy Spirit of God has made men to be shepherds (Acts 20:28). Elders exist because the words of the spirit direct the church, even giving a detailed character description of them. So when you are frustrated just stop and think about the parallel between you and elders and David and King Saul. Tread very cautiously every time you are confronted with these situations. Even elders who do not rule well are still worthy of single honor.

Having said that, think of ways you can give honor to all elders. You have a unique position in the church to praise them. Publicly give them credit for the many great decisions they make. There will be many in the church who will fail to honor elders, but you must not take part in those private conversations where members are not honoring elders. Never become part of those who degrade the elders. Listen to Solomon's wisdom and apply it to what you might be tempted to say privately. "Do not curse the king, even in your thought; do not curse the rich, even in your bedroom; for a bird of the air may carry your voice" (Ecc. 10:20). Rest assured that your words spoken privately against elders will rarely remain private!

Be the elders' cheerleader. Lead the congregation to have regard for them. The positive attitude you show toward the elders will become the attitude of the church. Defend them always for they have been anointed by God to be the shepherds. Your praise and special recognition of them is part of doing the work of an evangelist. God has told you to give double honor to some and single honor to all!

One final word about this. The rest of the passage in 1 Timothy shows that when sin is involved in the life of an elder you have the prime responsibility to deal with it. Never receive any accusation against an elder, but once sin has become obvious, God demands that you deal with it. If the elder does not repent of his sins, then courageously take the rest of Paul's instructions to Timothy. God will use you to rebuke a sinful elder in the presence of all, that the rest also may fear. Elders have great authority in the organization of the church and you occupy the place of checks and balances in His kingdom.

Spend Time With Your Elders

You will never develop a close relationship with your elders if you are only with them inside the church building. They must be your friends. The Lord spent so much time eating with people in His life and so should you. Think about how often the Bible mentions this. Use your home to practice hospitality and seek other avenues to get to know your elders well. Then when times of friction develop, their knowledge of you outside the building with vastly change how they treat you inside the building. The same holds true of your view of them. The time you spend with them outside the building enables you to understand why they make the decisions that impact the church. Conversations outside the building can help you develop a team spirit with them. Talk about it often, let them see you as someone on their side (how else could it be if you are both on the Lord's side), and work with them to develop goals for the church.

It is vitally important that you do not neglect getting to know the elders' families. Your greatest ally in the development of the church could easily be an elder's wife who has love and respect for you. Do all can to know as much as you can about the elders and their families.

A final word of caution. I strongly feel it is a mistake for you to develop a closer relationship with one elder than you do with the others. It so easily can happen for his interests and personality parallels yours so greatly. However, remember again something Paul said to Timothy about is work among elders: "I charge you before God and the Lord Jesus Christ and the elect angels that you observe these things without prejudice, doing nothing with partiality" (1 Tim. 5:21). Your work will progress much more smoothly if each of the elders sees you dealing the same way with each of them. This is a personal opinion and others may not agree with it, but I really believe you should have, as far as possible, the same relationship with all elders.

Behavior Inside the Meetings With Elders

How often you meet with the elders will not always be your decision, but your behavior inside those meetings has a lot to do with the relationship you have with them. Every situation is different, often varying from meeting to meeting, but there are some general principles you should keep in mind.

Recognize that you are not an elder. You are a preacher, a member of the church who is subject to the eldership. The reality is that this is equally true of all the elders. Every elder is individually subject to the entire eldership! Realizing that I am not an elder I have tried to always make sure every elder speaks about a particular matter before I say anything. The exception to this might be when they are discussing a matter and I have information they do not have (this by the way is why I think preachers should be part of most elders' meetings). Even then I try to back off and let them make the decision. If I speak early in the discussion I am acting like an elder. They are the shepherds and bishops and I serve under them. An added blessing from this approach is found in these words. "Even a fool is counted wise when he holds his peace; when he shuts his lips, he is considered perceptive" (Prov. 17:28).

You will be wise to often say, "God has given you the responsibility to make this decision and I promise you that whatever you decide will have my support and I will do all I can to make it succeed." God gave them that responsibility and I must not hinder their work nor minimize their authority before the church by anything I say or do inside or outside of the meeting. Such statements go a long way to help develop a good relationship with the elders. It helps them to see you as being part of team of leaders in the church.

Obviously, I am not talking about things that are sinful (elders must be aware that you are part of God's checks and balances when sin is involved). They need to be assured of your support. Verbalize your opinions when asked. Passionately plead for things about which you feel strongly, but let them know you are subject to their decisions.

One other important matter. You must never be the source of a leak of information which is obviously confidential. This is especially true when elders disagree over a matter. You should never say anything to anyone that indicates that not all the elders thought a matter should have been done. Preachers who have failed to do this have unwittingly sown discord and hindered the unity of the church. In this sense, you are part of the leadership of the church and your handling of these matters is critical. Elders need to present a united front on every decision when they leave the meeting and so should you.

When You are Fired

So you've been fired. My first response is, "Welcome to the crowd." Before getting all riled up about what has happened, stop and think about it for a few minutes. In many places this is how a congregation changes preachers. It may be that the relationship you have had with the elders and the congregation has changed, and you will be told that within a certain time frame they will no longer want you to serve the congregation. It may be much harsher than that and you are not treated (at least in your view) in a Christian way. Either way, you have to react to what has developed. What do you do?

Above all else, it is not a time to be overcome with evil (is that too harsh a word to describe what just happened?) and to return evil for evil. There will be those in the church who will be glad to see you go, but there will also be those who share you hurt. The worst thing you can do is to launch into a defense of yourself. You need to protect the Bride of Jesus above all else! Those who oppose you will not agree with you, and those who support you can become so polarized in defending you that the unity of the church is impacted for many months, if not years. It is extremely important that you protect your family, especially your children when you are fired. Probably, the wisest thing you can do is to do nothing, for whatever you do will likely harm the church. Be very careful what you say in the sermons you preach after people know you will be leaving. Your emotions will be heightened and you can say things you would not ordinarily say. Also those in the church can easily misunderstand what you say. So what do you preach? I would suggest you preach "first principle" sermons! The kind you would preach in a gospel meeting. This will help in avoiding any misunderstanding of your words. Take those weeks and focus on converting people you know. Work with the unchurched mates of members. Work with young people who love you but have not yet obeyed the gospel.

Just remember that within a few short months you will be in a new exciting work and things will likely be much better for you. If you stir up a mess just to settle a score before you leave, it may be months or years before things settle down again. Don't harm His beautiful bride just to make yourself feel better. Leave so peacefully that perhaps someday they will invite you back for a homecoming or to preach in a gospel meeting. His bride is far more important than the hurt you feel when you are asked to leave.

Final Thoughts

I am so glad you are a preacher. God had only one Son and He was a preacher. Before the world began God knew the church would exist and that preaching His truth would be part of His plan. Love preaching. Study diligently as long as you live. Take heed to the doctrine and to yourself. Let God use you. Fulfill your part in His eternal plan!

4

BUILDING RELATIONSHIPS WITH YOUNGER PREACHERS

Howard Norton

One measure of a football coach's career is the long-term success of his graduate assistants, assistant coaches, and coordinators after they leave his program. We think of great coaches like Bear Bryant of Alabama, Bud Wilkerson of Oklahoma, Frank Broyles of Arkansas, and Bobby Bowden of Florida State. Not only were these men successful as coaches; they developed coaches who became legends themselves.

What is true of sports is also true in other areas of life such as the military, business, industry, education, politics, banking, medicine, law, and—yes, the ministry of the word. Leaders who make a long-term difference do so by passing on their knowledge and experience to younger men who may become more influential and successful than those who inspired and taught them the ropes. Leaders whose influence lives on after they themselves have left the scene tend to practice two important truths.

One of these truths is an adage used often in conversations about foreign mission work. "A good missionary should work himself out of a job." All of us are temporary residents of earth just as Peter reminds us in his first epistle: "'All flesh is like grass and all its glory like the flower of grass. The grass withers, and the flower falls, but the word of the Lord remains forever.'" (ESV) Good missionaries and good local preachers are not people who create dependency on themselves and their personalities. Like parents of adult children, church leaders are successful when their immediate services are no longer required, and their followers are independent and able to stand on their own feet.

A conversation in Brazil with an internationally known agronomist and brother in Christ, Dr. John Murdock of the University of Wisconsin, indelibly printed the second truth on my mind when he said, "We must always remember that there is no success without successors." This sounds so much like Paul's exhortation to Timothy: "And what you have heard from me in the presence of many witnesses entrust to faithful men who will be able to teach others also." (ESV) Successful leadership in every phase of life is evident when those in the lead pass their knowledge, experience, and roles to prepared successors who will continue the struggle.

This chapter offers concrete suggestions concerning how older preachers can build relationships with younger preachers and pass the baton to them with as little disruption as possible in the local church and the brotherhood.

First, older preachers should make sure that their personal life and ministry are exemplary. 1 Timothy 4:16 has become an important text for younger preachers to follow when it says, "Keep a close watch on yourself and on the teaching." It is also an important text for older preachers. Young people can identify hypocrites and hirelings quickly—even when they are older. Unless an older preacher has his own life and ministry in order, younger men will pay little attention to his words of advice and will have virtually no desire to maintain a relationship with him.

Second, to build relationships with younger preachers, the older preacher must enjoy and appreciate the youthful worker. A Central American brother once said that in order for a North American to be an effective missionary in his part of the world, the missionary would need to understand the customs and culture of the country where he worked. He added, "And it would help if he also liked that culture." So it is with older preachers. If a man desires to make friends with and influence young preachers, it would really help to like them.

Third, older preachers who desire to build a good relationship with younger ministers must be transparent and vulnerable. I'm afraid some ministers are spooked by close fellowship with younger men because they fear their true selves will be discovered. In fact, working closely with a younger man opens an older preacher's life and ministry to public view. If he has lazy work habits, poor social skills, lack of ministry goals, questionable relations with the opposite sex, or a jealous spirit—whatever may be his situation—working with a younger preacher will show the man for what he is. On the other hand, an imperfect older preacher who is humble, submissive, and "like a nursing mother taking care of her own children" (ESV) will be loved in spite of his faults.

Fourth, building relationships with ministers of the next generation requires the older minister to appreciate the opinion of younger people. There is no question that differences of opinion will surface when fifty-year-olds are working side by side with young people in their twenties and thirties. While these differences present challenges, they also present great opportunities for both the older and younger worker. For the older man, he gets a close-up view of how the world he lives in is changing. The younger man, however, has the advantage of hearing a challenging point of view presented by a kind, mature friend whom he respects. The result is that everyone is stretched in his thinking. Being "brittle" is not a good characteristic for anyone. Inter-generational contact helps us stay flexible.

Fifth, impacting a young preacher's life requires the older man to have an open-door policy. C. E. McGaughey was one of the greatest evangelists of the twentieth century. I had the good fortune to work with him from January 1, 1958, until we moved to Brazil on June 1, 1961. He was a mentor par excellence. Without his coaching and encouragement, I'm not sure I would have made it in the ministry. One of his most endearing characteristics was that he truly loved younger preachers, and he was always available to visit with me when I needed to talk. I had plenty of questions, doubts, bad attitudes, and frustrations. He helped me work through them. It has now been fifty-four years since he mentored me. His influence is present every day I live and serve. I believe his loving, open-door policy was worth his investment of time and effort because "though he died, he still speaks" through me. If I want to serve beyond my death, I had better build relationships with people who will outlive me.

Sixth, it's important in building relationships with younger preachers to let them be young. We have no right to expect a twenty-three-year-old man to act like he's sixty-five. If he does, he'll have very little influence on his own generation; and he'll look weird to those of us who are older. Let a young person be young. This is difficult for people who do not interact with young people very much. I thank God that I've worked almost my entire life with young people. What a blessing! They are usually energetic, smiling, creative, optimistic, and eager to learn. They can also aggravate us. Still, they bless the life of older people who love them and are not afraid to let them be who they are. How they keep us young!

Seventh, to have a close relationship with young people, it is vital that older people maintain a good sense of humor. I worked for sixteen years with a great bunch of guys on the Sao Paulo Mission Team.They were full of fun. Two that stood out in this area were Glenn Owen and Don Vinzant. Both have now gone on to their heavenly home. Young and old alike loved these fellows because they were always smiling, liked to laugh, and made others laugh. They had a big influence on young preachers and young people in general, and much of that was due to their keen sense of humor. No one took human tragedy more seriously than they did, but they were also able to see the comedy in the daily routine of living. Young people adore older people who have a spring in their step and still get a kick out of life. It is difficult to get along with young people if a person can't laugh at himself and see humor in the things around him.

Eighth, being a friend of young preachers means we will recommend them. They probably don't know many people at the beginning of their public ministry and haven't learned how to go about seeking a ministry position. I remember that one of my biggest breaks came at the end of my senior year in college. Leonard Waggoner, preacher for the Broadway church in Houston, invited me to preach a Sunday morning sermon in his pulpit. Afterwards, he told Wyatt Sawyer, his preacher friend in the Pecan Park church, that my preaching had impressed him. A few days later, an elder from the MacGregor Park congregation mentioned to brother Sawyer that they were looking for a young man to serve as C. E. McGaughey's associate minister. It was then that Wyatt Sawyer told him about me, and I received the invitation to serve with brother McGaughey. Having an older minister who will put in a kind word at the right time can open doors for a young preacher in need of a boost.

Ninth, if they want to do mission work, younger preachers need leads and encouragement as they pursue financial support for their work. Men like C. E. McGaughey, Firm Foundation editor Reuel Lemmons, my preaching uncle, J. Willard Morrow, Fort Worth elder, Wade Banowsky, and many other older servants stuck their necks out for the Sao Paulo Mission Team to help us find funding. A Texas elder who suffered from blindness, Fletcher Dailey, Sr., accompanied me in the Houston area to vouch for our mission team and for me personally as we searched for funds. Bill D'Amico, another elder, helped me raise money to get to the field. His counsel and presence made an enormous contribution to our efforts, and I'll always be grateful for what he did. May the Lord bless the memory of all these wonderful older brothers who graciously did their work and then passed on to the other side.

Finally, older preachers build relationships by helping younger men identify their strengths and by offering guidance in their ministries. I had just graduated from Abilene Christian College in 1957 when I learned that I could drive in one day a week from Lingleville, Texas, and take two graduate courses. With my wife Jane's encouragement, I jumped at the opportunity. I had the good fortune to take a graduate-level Greek class under Dr. J. W. Roberts. Dr. Frank Pack, one of my generation's heroes, decided to audit the class. What a thrill to sit as a fellow-student with this brilliant scholar I admired so much. As the course came to an end and he learned that I would be moving away, he urged me to continue my studies. He said, "You have a good mind and the ability to do academic work. I want to encourage you to keep studying." Because of my admiration for Dr. Pack, that short conversation set me on a good path and inspired me to go forward. His confidence in me elevated my own. Older preachers have the capacity to do this for younger men when they help them see their talents, potential, and opportunities.

I have spent a major part of my life working with young people. It was always my desire to train young people for ministry even as others had trained me. The Lord Jesus Christ has allowed me to do this in different roles such as elder, youth minister, preacher, editor, missionary, teacher, preacher training school director, coordinator of evangelistic campaigns, and mentor. I thank God for this privilege and urge older preachers everywhere to embrace and befriend young people—especially young preachers. Let us encourage and inspire them, as Paul did the Corinthians, to "be steadfast, immovable, always abounding in the work of the Lord, knowing that in the Lord your labor is not in vain." (ESV)

6

USING MEDIA EFFECTIVELY

David Sain

The sounds and smell of breakfast being prepared made their way to my bedroom on that Sunday morning of August 16, as I took my time getting out of bed. We were living in Dexter, MO, where my father was the preacher for the Dexter Church of Christ. I was twenty years old, and I would soon be leaving home for my third year as a student at Freed-Hardeman College.

Shortly before 7:30, I heard the telephone ringing. A couple of minutes later, as she ended the phone call, my mother promised that she would do what she could about the matter. Then, she came to my bedroom and told me that the call was from KDEX, the local radio station, on which my father had a live weekly Sunday morning program, at 8:00. However, my father was out-of-town that Sunday, preaching in another state, and the station did not have a tape for that morning's broadcast. So, she asked me if I thought I could go to the station and speak in my father's place.

So I dressed hurriedly and drove to the station, thinking feverishly about what I could preach, what I should preach, and what I would preach. I decided to present a message that I had recently preached to a congregation in the area—a message that I thought would be appropriate for the potential audience, that I assumed would be comprised mostly of area residents, of various religious faiths. By God's grace and providence, I was able to meet that sudden opportunity and challenge. That was one of my earlier adventures in using the media in preaching. My first radio opportunity came one year earlier, when I was given the opportunity to speak on WAPO, in Chattanooga, TN, soon after finishing my first year at Freed-Hardeman. I remember how nervous I was as I took my seat in the studio, realizing how many hundreds of people could be listening—more people than I had ever spoken to at one time. Oh, what a responsibility, and, oh, what a great opportunity. Since those first experiences, I have been blessed with numerous opportunities to preach on radio, for the past fifty-five years, and on television for the past forty-six years. Those opportunities have included daily one-minute messages, daily five-minute programs, daily fifteen-minute programs, and weekly thirty-minute programs. Along the way, I sought and received good advice from media professionals, and I have tried to learn from brethren whom I consider to be the best in utilizing the vast world of media opportunities.

With personal experiences as a backdrop, and from the advice and examples of others, I offer the following observations and recommendations regarding the use of media in your work as a minister of the Gospel.

Expanding Our Horizons

What if you could preach the Gospel to 5,000 people every week? Would that excite you? Would it energize you? Of course, it would! Wow! Think about communicating your next sermon to more than 10,000 people! Well, that is possible in this day of amazing technology and electronic opportunities.

We live in a time that offers so many opportunities to reach people who seldom, if ever, step inside the church building to hear you preach from the pulpit. The avenues through which you can communicate with others are almost limitless—television, internet (websites, blogs, etc.), and social media (Facebook, Twitter, etc.). And, of course, there is still that effective means of reaching people through the printed page (books, tracts, journals, and articles in the newspaper and/or church bulletins).

The ability to communicate the Good News through the media means that we are not limited to the people who are physically present to hear our sermons on Sunday. The media allows us to expand our service as ministers of our Lord and Savior, and it is up to us to use it in spreading the Gospel.

More People Use Media Than "Attend Church."

The results of the surveys conducted by professional research groups (e.g., Barna Group) indicate that while more than half of adults in the United States attend a religious service in a typical month, a much larger percentage get religious information through some form of media in a typical month.

Radio and television, as well as religious magazines and books, remain popular sources of spiritual information and inspiration for millions of individuals. However, in the last two or three decades, faith-related websites, have become highly-used religious source, for millions of individuals.

• Thousands of adults listen to a Christian radio broadcast in a typical month.

• In a typical month, almost one-half of adults watch a religious television program.

• The internet search engines, and religious websites, are used more and more by people to obtain Biblical and religious information. And that includes a growing number of young people who are seeking answers for their inquiring minds.

• Obviously, the percentage of people making use of religious media is higher among religious people than among unchurched people. However, it would be a mistake to fail to include the unchurched in assessing the value of using the media to spread the Gospel. The number of adults in these United States who choose not to identify with any organized religion seems to be increasing, especially among the younger adults. While the majority of people are seldom, if ever, a part of our Sunday assemblies, and while many people will not invite us to enter their houses, physically, to study with them, the good news is that we can still reach them, through a website, a blog, the television, the radio, or the United States Postal Service.

Using the Media Effectively

1. Everyone loves a good story. In preaching the Gospel, we are telling the greatest story that can be told. Regardless of what method we are using, from the pulpit to the latest development of high-tech, let us never lose sight of what we are doing. We are telling the story about how God loved us, and gave his only begotten Son so that we can have everlasting life. We are telling the story of how God became one of us and sacrificed himself on the cross to make it possible for us to be forgiven of ALL of our sins. We are telling the

story of God's amazing, undeserved grace. We are telling the story that gives people joy, and peace, and hope! And, we need to tell that story with unfeigned love and compassion for everyone to whom we tell it.

2. Have a clear purpose. Have a clear focus for every message that you prepare and present. You should be able to distinctly and concisely state what your objective, your aim, is for each message, spoken or written—whether to a few people, or to thousands.

3. Do not take the easy way. Refuse to be content to draw from previous study or with a minimum effort. Be diligent in your planning, research, and studying. Also, write it or say it to the best of your ability. Do your best for the Master.

4. Stay in touch with culture. If you want to make an impact on those with whom you are communicating your messages, you need to understand the world in which they live. Understand their music. Know what they read. Be familiar with what they watch on television and in theaters. Stay informed about the latest trends, lingo, and styles. Your effectiveness in communicating God's Word will be greater if you are "in touch" with the world around you.

5. Know your audience. Before writing an article, consider who will most likely read it. Before you prepare a message for radio or television, consider who your audience most likely will be. Will it be mostly Christians, or non-Christians? What will be the

demographics of your audience? Are they young or old? Who will most likely comprise your audience at the time of your broadcast? Consult with the editors, the managers or officials to obtain helpful information regarding these matters.

6. Do not underestimate the importance of accuracy and quality. In writing and speaking, know what you are talking about. Quote accurately, and relate facts accurately. If you fail to do so, it discredits you and your message, and diminishes the effect of your message. Strive to use correct grammar. Incorrect grammar can distract from what you say, regardless of how true your words may be. Also, in broadcasting on radio or television, settle for nothing less than the very best quality in sound and appearance in every broadcast. Finally, in using the internet, do your best to have the state-of-the-art in layout, appearance, and user-friendly menu. Make every production (oral, printed, and electronic) one that is inviting.

7. Make it "Just you and me." In my personal judgment, the most effective use of radio and television is making the listener feel that you are talking personally to him or her. Years ago, I remember hearing Batsell Barrett Baxter on the Herald of Truth programs, and I thought he was outstanding in making you feel that it was just you and him—one on one—having a personal study. Sometimes, in describing what I am talking about, I use the phrase, "fireside chat." If you can achieve the effect of having

the listener feel that you are speaking directly and personally to him, I believe your message will make a greater impact upon him. This calls for the use of singular nouns and singular pronouns.

To facilitate this, you might find it helpful to visualize a person in your audience. Think of someone whom you believe is listening and see that person in the microphone or camera, and talk to that person. And to facilitate that, if someone tells me that he watches my television broadcasts, I tell him how much it encourages me to know that he watches, and then I tell him, "I am going to think about you when I record my next program." (I suspect that may affect how he listens to the message of the next program.)

Final Thought

You are blessed to be a minister of the Gospel when there are so many avenues open to you. Be wise and determine what outlets and resources you have to reach the greatest number of people. Including the pulpit, use every opportunity that you have, to preach the Word (2 Timothy 4:2).

7

HOW PREACHERS CAN HELP MEMBERS WHO ARE GRIEVING

Hardeman Nichols

Since the place of death pierces every mortal, it is necessary for all of us to learn how to handle bereavement. I have watched, with great admiration and respect, the courage that has borne many a saint through hours of sorrow. Here is some practical advice I have seen others use in dealing with grief.

1. Express your emotions. It should not be considered a Christian virtue to be unmoved by the loss of a loved one. There is a difference between suppressing one's emotions and losing one's self control. The Bible does

not say, "Sorrow not;" but it says, "Sorrow not as others who have no hope," (1 Thessalonians 4:13).

2. Seek the aid of your friends. The very presence of friends is encouragement. When Paul neared Rome, the brethren came to meet him and he "thanked God and took courage," (Acts 28:15).

3. Compel yourself to be with people. Your inclination may be to retreat into the refuge of privacy, but there is a greater need than one realizes to associate with others. David did (2 Samuel 12:19-23).

4. Express your feelings in words. Talking about it will help you to accept it. If this is done at the outset of bereavement, one will sooner be able to stabilize his life.

5. Avail yourself of spiritual resources. Even though you may not have realized the importance of the Scriptures and their comfort, now these can help in building your faith. The power of prayer and the peace of God are very precious possessions.

6. Don't brood over what might have been. Both Mary and Martha said, "If thou had been here my brother had not died" (John 11:21-32).

7. Actively pursue worthwhile tasks. Once the initial shock has been dealt with, get busy at other things. Resolve, like Paul, to "reach forth unto the things which are before," (Philippians 3:13).

8. Make careful and thoughtful decisions. Many an individual jumps hastily into deciding the full scope of the future rather than waiting until he has regained a proper perspective of life. Don't get in a hurry. Make prayerful decisions.

9. Increase your trust in God. Those who have come through their sorrows with a deeper faith can verify that God, Who rules over all, truly does make all things work together for good (Romans 8:28).

After the crises of grief, you can serve more fully and sympathize more completely with men of like passions. With Paul, you too can thank God for the comfort received, knowing that it has now given you the ability to comfort others who are in any trouble (2 Cor. 1:4).

8

THE PREACHER AND HIS MONEY

Jerrie Barber

Wise handling of money is a challenge and touches many facets of life. Jesus discussed it often. Here are some suggestions for fellow preachers.

"Don't trust anyone in a profession that begins with a "P": plumber, painter, policeman, or preacher."

That's a good example of prejudice. I've had it quoted to me many times. I'll listen to the statement a time or two with no response. Then I usually ask, "Do I owe you any money? Are you aware of anyone else to whom I am behind on my financial obligations? I am a preacher and have been for years. Perhaps a more accurate statement is, 'Some plumbers, painters, policemen, preachers AND doctors, lawyers, farmers, teachers, truck drivers, mechanics, accountants, housewives, and other human beings have trouble with money.' "

Talk About It

Money needs to be discussed before marriage. This topic provokes much conflict after marriage. Agreements we make before we get into a relationship reduce the conflicts after we get into the relationship.

In doing premarital counseling, I ask each person to complete a financial statement with all assets and liabilities on a spreadsheet, whether small or large. What do you own: cash, investments, car, house, real estate? What do you owe: car, house, student loans, credit cards? Without this full disclosure, you may, like Jacob, wake up with a different person from the one you thought you married.

Once you have the facts, it's good to discuss how to deal with what is, rather than what you wished it to be. Then you have the information to plan where you would like to go.

A family needs to stay current on finances. As I am writing this section, I just received a call from my wife. We agreed to "do our money" in an hour. Each week or two, we get together, record our transactions: income, spending in cards and cash, discuss upcoming expenses, and record them in our Quicken™ program.

Each month, we reconcile our accounts and budget for the next month.

We haven't always done it that way. When I first started preaching, I received $100.00 each week – total. We rented a house, paid the utilities, bought groceries, had no insurance (both babies were paid for in cash), and we didn't plan to retire. It was all covered with the $100.00 per week. We had a budget, made our expenses, gave liberally, didn't eat out much except when the brethren invited us, and it worked. We had an abacus-like calculator and kept accurate records. I still have the calculator and the books.

When we moved to the next church, we received $150.00 each week and a house was provided. We thought any family making $150.00 every week could spend whatever they wanted. So we didn't have a budget. We learned a powerful application of Paul's words, "Therefore let him who thinks he stands take heed lest he fall" (1 Corinthians 10:12).

I remember well the Saturday night when we spread cancelled checks, credit card receipts, bills, and despair all over the dining room table and painfully tried to start bringing back some order into our finances. We have been on a budget ever since. I make more than $150.00 each week and have since then. But I have never made enough to not need a budget.

Our regular conversations during "doing our money" provide an occasion to discuss all of life: God, the church, our children and grandchildren, opportunities to minister to others, our work, and our entertainment.

A child old enough to have money is old enough to start learning about money. When our children made money, we taught them to

1. Give some.
2. Save some.
3. Spend some.

The rule in our house was everyone gave on Sunday more than 10% of what they made the week before. Each child decided on their amount as long as it was above 10%. In our home devotionals, when we came to passages in the Bible relating to money and giving, we tried to make it practical to them. They knew how much we gave. When there were special contributions, we discussed how much more than our regular contribution we would be giving. They saved 10%. This was to be their college spending money.

When our children were thirteen years old, it was time for them to buy their own clothes. We still provided the money for their clothes, but we allotted to each one the monthly amount. Each was to shop, buy, and maintain his or her clothes. If they wanted to spend more, they could use their own money.

My wife, Gail, had the policy she would wash and dry the clothes. If they needed ironing, the child was to do it. I have good memories shopping with my son when he was in his early teens. We would go into a store. He would look for sales and examine the tag to see how much polyester was in the fabric to reduce or eliminate ironing.

A preacher and the church need to talk about money before employment. I like to be aware of who mentions it first. I am suspect of an elder or search committee member who opens with, "How much would it take to get you to move?".

Although I refuse to talk about money in the beginning, I am glad to talk about it before going to a new work. There need to be agreements on salary, housing allowance, insurance, expenses to lectureships, amount of time off for conducting meetings, expenses for making the transition from one congregation to another, and vacation. I like to have two clauses on increases in compensation:

1. A cost-of-living adjustment will be made each year. If there are not adjustments, most years you are getting a decrease. A regular cost-of-living adjustment keeps you even with where you started.

2. A merit raise will be considered each year and discussed as to why it is being given or not given. I want this discussion each year. Sometimes the discussion is worth more than the money. One eldership had my evaluation each year the week before my anniversary in coming to the congregation. They listed everything I had done right and commendable during the last twelve months: helpful sermons, memorable classes, programs or personal initiatives that blessed individuals or the congregation. I looked

forward to my evaluation each year and could hardly wait to get home and read it to Gail. After this, they told me about my merit raise. I appreciated both the discussion and the money.

I've had to remind elders about the contract, my evaluation, and raises. Often the joy of courtship fades after a year or two. Many have not practiced this and will forget. This is one reason agreements need to be written. People forget. Two observations:

1. People receiving money or benefits have better memories than people paying money.

2. The only people who don't need written agreements are people who will never die and will never forget.

I want to know when, where, and how I will be paid. I endured eight years and four months of humiliation of being paid every Sunday morning in the foyer before Bible study. The treasurer would hand me my check in an envelope in front of all who were there. Then the comments would begin: "Where's mine?" "How much is it?" "Why can't I have a check?" "I wish I got paid for working an hour a week."

I am embarrassed I was too scared to make a correction to something I dreaded each week. The treasurer was a good man who helped and encouraged my family and me while we worked there. The ones making the comments were good people. My guess is they thought it was funny. I hated it. A few years later, I learned to talk like an adult to other adults. Since then, when I am discussing details about working with a new congregation, I ask when, how often, where, and how I can expect to receive my salary.

Do Something About It

People will know how I handle money. I have the choice of my stewardship being a part of a good example or a stumbling block. I like to give liberally. God will know and respond. People will know. The people who count the money will know. Brethren will notice whether I put something into the collection plate or not.

I have never seriously considered the advice I've heard about saving on taxes by agreeing on a salary, reducing the salary by the amount you plan to give, and since you never received it, you'll not have to pay income tax and social security on the amount of the contribution. I have always thought my example was worth the price of the tax.

It's been my practice to pay bills early. Then, if they're a little late, they're still on time. It's like arriving early for all appointments. My father had a policy of leaving home in time to have a flat tire. If we didn't have a flat tire, we'd be early. If we had a flat tire, we'd still be on time.

People know. People notice. People talk. How we handle money will have an influence on our ministry.

Get started early on long-range financial plans. If you haven't already started, now is the earliest time you have.

It's easier to add something to something than to start something from nothing. Early in my life I would start a saving account. I would add to it. Then when I was ready to buy a car, I'd ask myself, "Why should I borrow money and pay interest on it when I have money in savings not paying the amount of interest I'll be paying on my car?" I would then empty my saving account. I finally realized if I were ever to have an emergency fund or a retirement account, I had to get started and leave it alone.

Grow in Your Stewardship

To be effective in any area, one has to know the fundamentals. I know of no better approach than the principles taught by Dave Ramsey. His current book is The Total Money Makeover. There are classes called Financial Peace University. You can take it online, individually, or in groups in churches and other public places. Gail and I attended this training several years ago when Dave was teaching it live at the Holiday Inn in Brentwood, Tennessee. We added what we learned there to what we had been practicing. I now recommend during premarital counseling for each couple to go through this material together and decide how they will handle their money after marriage.

One of the principles is to eliminate debt. We paid off our car and instead of trading for another we started paying ourselves a car payment each month to buy our next car. I trade cars when it costs half as much to repair as the car is worth. When I've been making car payments to myself, I know how much I can afford to spend. I am committed to save to buy cars. I don't get sick each time I trade cars as I used to when I signed a note for years of payments to buy at high interest a product swiftly decreasing in value.

I didn't do this until later in life. I wasted thousands of dollars on new cars and interest until I committed to cash only. To reach any goal, four things are necessary:

1. Determine where you are.
2. Decide where you want to go.
3. Devise a plan to get there.
4. Do it.

I remember our family going to Helen, Georgia, on our annual Operation Forward trip. That year I wrote a plan to get us from our situation then to a place where we could pay for our house and set aside a specific amount for retirement. I monitored the plan each year to encourage us to stay on track. I personally enjoy putting this information on a spreadsheet and making charts to see the progress.

During the time I was getting out of debt and going toward my goals, I needed to provide for my family in case I became disabled or died before I reached my goals.

The general rule is to insure what you can't afford to lose. If I am not financially secure, I can't afford to lose my health or my life for the sake of my family. To provide for this, I bought disability insurance and life insurance. Once a person accumulates some assets, some say a net worth of $25,000.00 or more, it's good to buy an umbrella policy to protect your liability above those included in a standard auto or homeowner's policy.

During the years, I've found trusted people who have told me what they thought I needed, gave me time to think, and assisted me when I was ready to buy. I never turned all my finances over to one specific individual. I always studied, thought, and used ideas from several people to decide the best course to take.

Enjoy the Process and Remember the Goal

Jesus promised when we put His kingdom first, He will provide the necessities of life. Our opportunity is to be good managers of everything God has entrusted to us.

I enjoy setting goals and reaching them. I've found it helpful to monitor my progress in finances. I remember signing the note for our first house. It seemed like such a long time before we would be debt free. I drew a chart with each payment represented by a square. I looked forward each month to coloring the square red, corresponding to the payment. After a few years, I noticed we were approaching the halfway point. We talked with our children and discussed where we would like to go for a Half-Paying-for-our-House Party. They selected a fun restaurant in Chattanooga and we enjoyed the night, thanking God and feeling good about the progress we had made.

Although money is not the most important thing, it is important. Jesus said money will lead to where our heart will be. I used to tell people if their attitude were right, they would give. That's true. However, Jesus taught to not only invest in things on earth but to make heavenly investments a priority for, "Your heart will always be where your treasure is" (Matthew 6:21, CEV). He said that money leads the heart.

May God bless us to use everything He gives us to His glory.

If I can be helpful to you in this, or any other area, please contact me:
www.newshepherdsorientation.com
jerrie@barberclippings.com

9

THE PREACHER AND HIS EDUCATION

Stafford North

I appreciate the opportunity to participate in this project. I began preaching when I was a sophomore in college, in 1948. That was 67 years ago. Time passes pretty quickly. My role at Oklahoma Christian has allowed me to be involved in the preparation of many for the ministry and that has been a great blessing.

A preacher must be educated. There are truths he must know and he must know how to present them. Jesus trained His apostles for three years and then gave them the Holy Spirit to tell them what to say (Luke 12:12; John 16:13). And after Paul was converted, he appears to have gone to Arabia for two years for preparation to do his work (Galatians 1:17). If these men needed to be educated for their next work, certainly those today who want to preach need to prepare. What is the best way for one to prepare for preaching?

I guess we have all heard of those who prepared themselves by their own study. While not as likely today as it once was, a person can read and practice on his own and learn what he needs to know. He is more likely to learn these things, however, if he completes some type of training program where experienced people have put together a curriculum and who have preached for many years guide students through it. Some choose to go to a school of preaching often with a two-year intensified program to learn the Bible and the skills of preaching. Such schools have trained many.

Others attend Christian universities with four-year programs including study in the Bible and preaching skills, also studying other subjects such as writing, speech, history, science, psychology, and literature.

What are some specific things a person preparing to preach should learn? The easy answer is "everything." Continual learning from the scriptures and those who write about them is essential. Some preachers use movies or novels or poems from which to draw examples or illustrations. Others make good use of sports in their preaching. Still others find examples from real life experiences which they weave into their lessons. One preacher I know reads the Sunday New

York Times each week to stay abreast of what is going on in the world of politics, literature, sports, and world affairs to enable him relate his sermons to issues important in our culture.

The preacher's education should never stop; for if it does so, his message will grow stale.

1. The preacher needs to be educated in the scriptures.

The more the preacher knows about the message of the Bible the better, but here are some fundamental things he should know. He needs to know the "story" of the Bible so he can fit the pieces together. Ephesians 3:9 speaks of the "mystery" which God developed step by step from before creation and which culminated in the church.

One can see this mystery unfolded through the story and predictions of the Old Testament and then in their fulfillment by Jesus' coming, death and resurrection, and in the establishment and spread of the church. Knowing this "thread" that runs through scripture will enable the preacher to tie the pieces together.

The preacher also needs to know the "heart" of the message in all the Bible books. This element could well include some memorization of key scriptures that capture the essential elements in various books. Knowing these books will help him develop sermons that utilize key scriptures well. Being educated in scripture also includes knowing the Bible characters and their stories as well as the periods through which the Bible takes us.

2. The preacher needs to be educated in the fundamental doctrines of the Bible.

Knowing the Bible well will enable the preacher to know much about the doctrines of the Bible, but he also needs to know these doctrines in a way that will enable him to teach his congregation about them and defend these concepts in classes and in his personal teaching. A partial list of such doctrines would include: the nature of the trinity and how each works in our lives today, sin with its consequences, the function and place of the law of Moses in the plan of God, prophecies about Jesus and their fulfillment, atonement through the sacrifice of Jesus, the resurrection of Jesus, the establishment of the church and how it fits into the purpose of God, and the response we must make to God's offer of salvation through faith, confession, repentance, and baptism. He also needs to know about the organization and work of the church, the worship of the church, the moral principles which God expects us to follow, the ultimate return of Jesus to raise us from the dead to bring us to the final judgment, and the eternal punishment of the unsaved and the reward of the saved. In all of these great truths and others as well, the preacher must be well educated.

The preacher should be well-grounded in all of these doctrines so he may include them in his preaching to teach his congregation about them. In addition, he must also be able to recognize when people are presenting false teaching in these fundamentals of the faith and, in such cases, he must be able to refute them. Being competent in these basic doctrines is an essential element of the work of the preacher.

3. The preacher needs to be educated in hermeneutics.

Knowing the principles of properly interpreting scripture and having good practice in using them is essential in the education of the preacher. As the preacher prepares his sermons and Bible classes and in articles he writes, he will be making frequent reference to scripture. When he does, he must know how properly to draw the meaning from a passage. To interpret scripture properly, the preacher must be experienced in such principles as these: knowing who wrote the passage and to whom it was written; the conditions under which the passage was written including the situation, history, geography, archaeology, and culture; how to deal with context, genre, word meanings, syntax, and the use of figurative language; how the passage fits into the broader theology of scripture; what light other passages can shed on the one he is studying; and how to make appropriate applications of the passage to our time, place, and circumstances.

The preacher should be trained in hermeneutics early enough in his educational experience that when he his taking more advanced courses in the Bible text, he can practice using what he has learned in how to interpret a text. Using proper principles to glean the meaning of a passage is essential to the work of the preacher.

4. The preacher must be educated in homiletics.

There have been those who were well versed in scripture and yet who were not able to present it well to an audience. Perhaps they had not thought about the needs of the audience or they did not present the message in a clear or understandable fashion. We hear such expressions as "that was over my head," "I never got what he was driving at," or "I heard him but I don't know what to do with it."

In order for the preacher to do well, then, he must have training in the principles of the preparation and delivery of sermons. That means that he knows how to suit his lesson well to his audience and can bring messages that deal with their spiritual needs. He can analyze a passage for an expository sermon and can use effectively other forms of sermon organization so the people can follow the message as it unfolds. He knows how to use scriptures and other materials to develop the sermon and especially knows how to motivate with effective examples and appeals. He can speak with clarity, directness, and fervor, and can make good use of his body language as he preaches.

And most important of all, he can make practical applications that will help his audience put into practice the message he brings from scripture. Learning to make effective use of these principles can enable a preacher to serve much more effectively.

5. The preacher must be educated in apologetics. There will be attacks on the scripture from many directions and the preacher must be prepared both to defend the Bible and to teach others to do so. He must be taught to believe in and to explain the inspiration and inerrancy of the scriptures and to demonstrate that the Bible story of creation is correct.

He needs to know how archaeological discoveries support the Bible and how to deal with the charges of errors in scripture. He needs to know how the canon was developed and the history of Bible translations. And he needs to know how to deal with issucs often brought against Christianity such as the problem of evil and suffering, how could a loving God send people to hell, and what about the mistakes so called Christians have made through the years.

6. The preacher must be educated in world religions.

We live in a multi-cultural society where people hold many different religious views. Not only are there a wide variety of views among those claiming to believe in Jesus, but there are an increasing number in the United States who believe in such religious as Islam, Hinduism, Scientology, and even Satan-worship. If one is going to be prepared to relate to the culture and prepare people to do the same, he must be acquainted with these various religions. He should be able to compare their basic beliefs with those of Christianity to show the similarities and differences. Of course, he needs to be able to show ways in which Christianity should be preferred over other options.

7. The preacher must be educated in Restoration History.

Today's preacher must be taught that the church began on the Day of Pentecost and that those doctrines the apostles taught and what they led the early church to practice established the model God wanted His people to follow for all ages to come. They need to understand what this teaching was as it deals with such matters as how to be saved, how the church is to fellowship, serve, and worship, and how the church is to be organized.

The preacher also needs to know how the apostles predicted that the church would depart from what the scripture describes as the apostles' teaching, the truth, the faith, and the gospel (Acts 2:42; 1 Timothy 4:1-3; Romans 1:16; Acts 20:28-29). He then should be able to explain how this departure took place over the years and then how some brave men sought to reform some of these practices and how other courageous men led in a restoration effort. They need to know that this Restoration Movement was not seeking to establish a new denomination, but that it sought to go back beyond denominations to the point of just being the early church again.

If the preacher does not understand this concept, he will not know how to deal with the problem of denominations and will not be encouraging people to believe what the apostles taught and what the early church practiced. Young preachers should be taught to say, "We do this because that is how the early church did it." This understanding will help them deal with many of the issues in the church today such as whether baptism is essential to salvation, whether women should be allowed to lead in worship, and whether we should use instruments in worship. The simplest answer to these questions often is, "Let's just do it like the early church did. We know that is right and we can't be sure that some other way is right."

8. The preacher should be educated in how to deal with people.

The preparation and delivery of his weekly sermons is an essential part of the preachers' work. Through these messages he can educate the church in the essential things they should know as well as motivate and inspire them to serve the Lord. But few preachers have preaching as their only responsibility. They have to deal with people. They must know how to work with elders, how to teach individual Bible studies, how to help those who are in grief and distress, how to provide first-level counseling, how to advise those with spiritual problems.

Preachers work with people. They preach to them, they visit them, they share their joys and sorrows, they learn from them. No preacher can do his work well without dealing with the people of the church and the people of the community. His education, then, would not be complete without some preparation in this essential work of the preacher.

Some of this education comes in classes he takes but much of it comes through his dealing with people in job situations, social clubs, athletics, student activities, campaigns, and other similar experiences.

So, the preacher's education in a school that prepares ministers is a vital step in his preparation. Some get their education at a bachelor's degree level and a growing number pursue it through graduate training. Their education needs to be thorough and it needs to deal with all of these essential elements. Preachers must understand that their education is never complete. They must have a mind open to learning from studying the Bible, keeping up with the world around them, and being in touch with people. A preacher must never think he is through with his education.

10

HOW TO WORK WITH ONE CHURCH OVER A LONG PERIOD OF TIME

Robert K. Ogelsby, Sr.

Just a personal word from this author before we start the chapter. I may never know you, and you may never meet me, but as you read this chapter, you and I are going to have something that resembles a father-to-son chat about preaching. The remarks I will share with you are based on two things; that is, my study of Scripture and my experience of ministering 52 years in the same church.

Before you reject these suggestions, just remember that I have discarded the things that did not work for me. This means that what I am sharing with you are the insights I have found most valuable in ministry. In a sense I am trying to pass on to you what has proved to me to be "the pearl of great price."

Somewhere in your preparation for ministry, you will include academic training. Most ministers come out of their formal schooling with a good theoretical basis for ministry. Those who teach you will likely do an excellent job of equipping you with the tools you will need for ministry.

A good academic education will help you to have a better career in ministry. May I warn you, however, that not many ministers are ever fired because they did not master Greek. Likewise, few are dismissed because they do not teach the truth. In some cases, brethren may even be willing to endure less than perfect delivery of sermons in the pulpit.

What most ministers are not prepared for is that they may run aground on purely practical problems.

First, in our time together we will talk about survival in the first few years of ministry. It will do us no good to speak of staying at one church a "long time," if you cannot successful survive the first critical years of ministry. It makes no difference where you begin your ministry, how old or young you are, or whether you are a beginner or a veteran. If you cannot survive the first practical tests, your ministry will not survive long enough to become an extended ministry in one church.

The suggestions I will share with you are not many in number, and none of them are out of your reach.

The only qualification to my advice is that you should "give it a try." Enough said about that–let's get started.

1. Discover your ministry description from the first day.

The first thing all ministers need to know before they begin work with a congregation is, "What will be my ministry task at this church?" Preachers are expected to answer interview questions asked by an eldership. The elders therefore wind up knowing a lot about the minister, but the minister often knows next to nothing about the leadership's expectations.

Rest assured the church leadership has expectations of you, even though they will often be unspoken. In the early stages of a ministry, this will make little difference because you are in a "honeymoon period" in which mistakes are overlooked. Later, those misunderstandings may become crucial, and in some cases develop into a terminal illness for your ministry.

So get your ministry description in writing. That can be simple to say and difficult to do but there is an easy solution.

Your first step is to discuss your ministry description with the church leadership. They may act as if this is not necessary. They may even say "Don't worry. We trust you. We all know (more or less) what your ministry is." At a later date, those comforting words may seal your ministry's doom. Since it is so important to your success, it will be up to you to courteously request their permission to ask them some questions. Only by this method can you uncover preconceptions that even they don't know they have.

Your second step will be to transform spoken words into a more permanent written record. That is not as difficult as it may sound. Before you start your questions, you should ask their permission to make some notes. Those notes should be brief ones taken during the discussion which follows. Then, as soon as you leave the meeting, expand your brief notes into a more complete written description.

Your third step will be to mail a copy of your notes of ministry understanding to each and every elder. This should be in the form of a friendly letter. You should begin by saying, "This is my tentative understanding of what we discussed." Spell out your understanding of what you heard. Put each elder's name on his copy. Then if someone fails to pick up his copy, it will be obvious which one did not get the message. Only later will you discover the value of making sure each elder receives his own copy.

At the bottom of your letter, ask them to correct anything which you have misunderstood and add anything you have omitted.

Your problem now shifts to finding a way to get the corrections in writing. If they call on the phone, make notes of the corrections, incorporate them into the modified letter and send them an updated copy. Date the new version of the letter of understanding and mention the name of the person who gave you the corrections.

What is the value of that step? It simply means if misunderstandings arise in the future, this written document will establish who has the poor memory. Few people deliberately distort an agreement, but memories do fade (even yours!) with time. This letter will not be a binding legal contract, but it will help keep your ministry on course and avoid the "blame game" later. This signed and dated letter will be your wall of protection. Future discussions about your ministry task will be shortened with this kind of record.

2. Track your ministry time before the crisis.

Your second consideration is how well you use your time once you have joined the ministry team. With the passing of time you will discover the use of your time is a very subjective question. Any discussion of efficient time use will quickly lapse into a "you said....I said" quandary. How does one prevent the rigors of that crisis?

The best defense against your own bad perception and that of others is something called a daily log or an appointment book. You keep it on your desk at all times. Write brief notes in it, describing what you did during each time period of your day.

That daily log will do wonders for you when you're in "hot water." At such times, you don't have to guess what you did. You can open your daily log and read it to refresh your memory, and theirs. Notes in this log do not have to be complicated. They do, however, need to be accurate.

The first cry that goes up from ministers who have never kept a log is, "I am so busy doing God's work that I don't have time to keep a log." First of all, we are not talking about a time consuming ledger. We're talking about brief notes quickly written. How much time does it take to write the word "counseling" on your log? How long will it take you to enter the name of someone you visited in your hospital log? So objecting to a log is usually a matter of resisting change or perhaps not wanting to be transparent with those who supervise your work.

That daily log procedure can easily morph into a brief one page monthly report. A month is easy to summarize once you have a week by week running account of your time schedule. You will be amazed at how clearly your ministry is summarized by this simple record. Doing this all year long will give you a wonderful ministry record for your whole year. The monthly report will probably require one hour or less. In light of the benefits it gives you, it is an excellent investment of your time.

Like one building block on another, the daily log and the monthly reports open up a new opportunity. You can scan those twelve monthly reports and create an annual review for the activities of a whole year. This means you will automatically be ready for that dreaded annual review. With your yearly log printed and under your arm, you will be relaxed and ready for your review. You can give each elder a copy of your year's activities. One result will be that both you and your spiritual overseers may be pleasantly surprised at how much you have accomplished in a year. That impression in itself makes possible a highly favorable report of your work record for the year. Such a record may indeed lengthen your stay at that congregation.

3.Learn to work with people.

The first two suggestions we have given you will get you started in ministry, but other strategies are necessary in order to "stay the course." Even though you successfully complete your first years at a church, you will still find it a challenge to stay there for more years.

Much of what you do in ministry will be informal. You will publicly preach in the pulpit and teach in the classroom, but your biggest task will be learning how to work with people in smaller groups. Whether you realize it or not, every church is composed of a series of small informal groups. This means you need to learn the dynamics of small groups. You will need to learn why Elders' meetings function as they do. When lecture teaching doesn't work, you need an alternate teaching method, such as teaching with questions and discussion. Also, conflict will happen. You would like to avoid it, but you can't. You, therefore, need some skill in conflict management. Learn the dynamics of small groups and you will be a victor. Fail to learn it, and you will be a victim.

This particular suggestion is too lengthy to fit into a chapter. Some general guidelines are that you should practice paying careful attention to everything happening around you. Be curious and learn to ask questions. Remember, you are on a life-long journey of learning. In spite of your graduation and your formal college degrees, life has much more to teach you about ministry. As much as I would love to describe the strategies of how to solve these problems, it cannot be done in just one chapter of a book. If you have specific questions in this field, the author invites you to write your questions to him at Waterview Church of Christ, 1409 N. Waterview Drive, Richardson, Texas 75080 or send e-mails to him at church@waterview.org. Any material mailed to you will be free.

4. Balance in ministry.

The ultimate secret of a successful long term ministry can be captured in one word—Balance. It's a short word and easy to remember. Staying in balance will lengthen your ministry, and falling out of balance will shorten it. If you want to last a long time in one church, you cannot afford that mistake, because it will be your undoing. You may ask, "Balance in what?"

Balance in Teaching

Keep records of what you preach and teach. Check yourself often. Note the "ruts" you fall into. It may be repeating your favorite subjects too many times. It may be getting stuck in one style of presentation. It may be shying away from difficult or unpopular subjects. Resist the "rut tendency." If you plan to preach lots of sermons to essentially the same audience, then you must keep a sermon log and balance the spiritual diet you feed the congregation.

Balance in Your Time

How are you spending your time? There's that daily log suggestion again. You may think you are doing fine, but check the balance on your records. As sure as the sun coming up in the morning, someone will sooner or later accuse you of misusing your time. Watching out for the time "ruts" will help you to correct that tendency.

Balance in Social Activity

It is also important to keep your social life in balance. Are you spending too much time with one group in the church? Do you find one friend especially encouraging? Watch out. Jealousy will arise from others. Remember, you are to minister to everyone, not minister, not just a few special friends. You don't think that will cause trouble? Come back after two years of ministry and tell me about it! You may protest that you need special friends. Of course you do, but if you plan to stay long in one congregation, you must balance your need with the good of the church. Yes, I know Jesus had close friends. Peter, James, and John had special places with him on the mount of transfiguration and in the garden of Gethsemane. How did Jesus get away with it? It may be because he loved all of his disciples and never flaunted his special love for the few. You can take care of your personal needs by having appropriate friendships outside your congregation.

After all these suggestions, you may not want to pay the price of staying a long time in one church! So why even consider it? The answers are many. A long time in one church builds trust, enlarges influence, and gives you tools to accomplish things for God.

What about the Ministerial Staff?

Everything that's been said about the minister and congregation also applies to the ministerial staff. All the suggestions we have made apply to staff ministers as well. Keeping a log of daily time use, making monthly reports, and doing annual summaries will pay rich dividends with everyone. Using your records to keep balanced and out of "ruts" will definitely lengthen your ministry in any church. Clear records will make staff conflicts much easier to handle.

Now don't let all this advice discourage you. My 60 years in ministry have been fulfilling, and I would do it all over again. I share these guidelines with you in the hope it will make your ministry more productive and satisfying. It has transformed my ministry. I send it forth with a prayer it will enrich yours as well.

11

THE NEED FOR PREACHERS TO WRITE

Cecil May, Jr.

Preachers preach, that's what we do. In addition some preachers also write: bulletin articles, articles for publication in the local newspaper, articles for publication in brotherhood papers, books and blogs. It is a trend to be encouraged. It is good for the church, good for those outside the church who may never have a chance to hear a particular preacher in person, and it is good for the preacher himself.

A needed caveat! Ministry is not one-size-fits-all. Scripture, in 1 Corinthians 12 and Romans 12, calls us to recognize that there are different tasks and functions, and for that reason Christians differ in talents and abilities. Some preachers have a knack for engaging an audience conversationally. Some are dynamic. Some can unravel complexities and make them simple. Some are just better organizers and speakers than others. A visitor to a congregation where the preacher wrote out his sermons in full manuscript form and then read them from the pulpit was asked later what he thought about the presentation. He replied, "Not too good: For one, he read his sermon; secondly he didn't read it very well; and third, it wasn't worth reading."

Jesus reminds us, though, that unused and undeveloped talent can be enhanced by usage. The principle, "use it or lose it" (Matt. 25:29), has a corollary: "use it and improve it." It is "a faithful saying and worthy of all acceptance" that "practice makes perfect." No one should just decide, "I have no talent for speaking or for writing," without trying. If after trying you decide either speaking or writing or both is not "you," there are many other effective ways to serve the Lord.

Good for the Church

If Alexander Campbell, B. C. Goodpasture, Furman Kearley, Earl West, and many others had not left their writings to inform and inspire us, we would be much poorer. Personally, I have been heavily influenced from the beginning of my preaching by written works of the following preachers: 1) J. W. McGarvey's Sermons, especially his sermons on cases of conversion in Acts and on providence from Old Testament narratives; 2) G. C. Brewer's Sermons and Foundation Facts and Primary Principles, preaching Christ crucified; showing the biblical connection between faith and obedience and between law and grace and the biblical concept of undenominational Christianity; 3) Thomas Campbell's Declaration and Address; and 4) Barton W. Stone's Last Will and Testament of the Springfield Presbytery. I could, of course, add many others to the list.

I may have been asked to write this chapter of this book because of a recent decision I made to write more. At 80 (83, now) I was feeling my mortality. I am concerned for a sound (balanced) presentation of "the whole counsel of God" (Acts 20:27), and there are some particular emphases I want to encourage because I sense they are largely neglected. I felt time was running out. I wanted to put them in print because I am likely not going to be able much longer to continue preaching them orally.

Some may decide to preach, or write, and then think of something to say. The best preachers and writers have something that needs to be said and they, therefore, must preach or write.

"If I say, 'I will not mention him, or speak any more in his name,' there is in my heart as it were a burning fire shut up in my bones, and I am weary with holding it in, and I cannot" (Jeremiah 20:9).

"For if I preach the gospel, that gives me no ground for boasting. For necessity is laid upon me. Woe to me if I do not preach the gospel!" (1 Corinthians 9:16).

"But Peter and John answered them, 'Whether it is right in the sight of God to listen to you rather than to God, you must judge, for we cannot but speak of what we have seen and heard' " (Acts 4:19-20).

Following are the themes heavy on my heart impelling me to write. What impels you is probably different, but it should be something.

Most preachers I am hearing believe in the preeminence of Christ and Him crucified as the foundation of the gospel message, but it seems to me too often assumed rather than emphasized, and for the sake of the hearers in the pew it needs constant repetition. We say the church is non-denominational, but we often sound as if we are encouraging people to seek and find the right denomination and become a member of it (we would not say "join it") to be saved.

Some emphasize right assembly worship to the neglect of justice, mercy and faithfulness; others say the only way to get us to practice mercy and justice is to abandon the idea of correct assembly worship; Jesus says we need both (Matt. 23:23). Those are not the only things I write about, but I consciously try to keep them in the forefront.

Others may have different things they feel are neglected. Whatever it is, writing is a good way to help correct that.

Many churches produce bulletins. Try writing a teaching article each issue. Write according to your sense of the need. Some write to admonish and edify the church; some tend to write for the benefit of those not yet Christians, some write to correct brotherhood problems.

Develop a mailing list of people who are interested in the kind of things you are writing about. Feedback from that audience will help you decide whether or not writing is for you. That explains my motivation for writing. Good writers desire to reach more people over a longer period of time. Good writing does that.

Good for Those outside the Church

Preaching reaches, for the most part, those whom we can entice to come into our buildings. Other options need to be used to reach outside the building. Television and radio are among the possibilities, but so is writing. Regular teaching ads in the newspaper can be effective. In most cases what I call "ice-breaker" ads are more effective than articles proving the necessity of baptism or the importance of a cappella singing. Articles that address moral issues or that advocate biblical family values will often be read and appreciated and can help create a climate that encourages people to attend our services or to be attentive to later more direct articles on religious differences. The New Testament epistles exemplify the value of beginning on common ground before moving on to fundamental differences.

Attractive, well-written articles of that sort may sometimes be accepted for print without charge. They open minds and hearts to be ready to consider later articles that may be more controversial or thought-provoking.

Good for the Preacher

Writing is also good for the writer. Sir Francis Bacon's well-known quote is true: "Reading maketh a full man; conference a ready man; and writing an exact man."

By "conference" he means discussion and dialogue. Writing does drive one toward precision of thought and exactitude of expression, traits which help clarify what is received by reading and imparted by confidence.

There are three steps to good writing and it is good to work deliberately through the three step process.

Step 1: Decide What to Write.

This decision may be precipitated in a number of ways. An idea may already be burning in your heart and need expressing. An idea may come to mind most any time for a useful article. It may come at 3:00 o'clock in the morning during a brief waking moment, or while hearing someone preach or teach, or while reading an article or book. Seize the idea. Do not let it escape. Keep a pen and paper handy, or make an iPhone note. For some the idea may come in the form of an assignment.

At this point there are similarities between writing and preaching. Read and study materials related to the chosen theme. Develop a case for what you want to accomplish. Find some helpful illustrations and do not overlook Scripture as an excellent source of illustrations. Consider and collect relevant Bible verses.

Another caveat here! There is a temptation to ignore context and twist words to make Bible verses say what we want them to say. Be sure your point is true to the total biblical message and, if it is not, choose another point.

Step 2: Write.

Write on the topic in "stream of consciousness" style. Write like you would talk. Make your best persuasive case without worrying much about grammar and style. Very important: consider this your first draft, not your final product.

Step 3: Rewrite, rewrite and rewrite.

This is the step that separates writing from preaching. Read to correct any grammar mistakes. Speaking is not as formal as writing. For example, contractions (isn't, don't, shouldn't) are inappropriate in formal writing and most writing should follow formal style. One read-through should be for the express purpose of eliminating excess wordage.

This rewriting step is where "writing (makes) an exact man" takes place. It is my experience that the precision good writing requires carries over to some degree in our speaking. Most poor writing I have seen gives the impression that the first draft was sent in as the finished product. Writing affords the luxury of presenting a more polished product than is usually possible with speaking. Taking advantage of that opportunity makes for both a better finished writing product and ultimately an improved speaker.

12

FAITHFULNESS OVER THE LONG HAUL

Hugh Fulford

"No one, having put his hand to the plow, and looking back, is fit for the kingdom of God" (Luke 9:62).

"Before I go," I would like to encourage all who have entered and all who will enter the magnificent work of preaching the glorious gospel of Christ to steel themselves for faithfulness over the long haul. It is one thing to enter the ministry of the word and later discover that one really is not prepared (spiritually, educationally, temperamentally, or otherwise) for this work and therefore make a gracious exit from the work, and another thing to allow the cares of this world to cause him to abandon the ministry. (Tragically, Demas was not the last preacher to forsake the cause of Christ because of a love for this present world [2 Timothy 4:10]). Still worse, is the tragedy of attempting to remain in ministry when one no longer has the heart for it, and is simply going through the motions of serving as a preacher but with no verve, no excitement, no joy, and no satisfaction from what he is doing. So, how does one prepare himself for faithfulness over the long haul in the work of ministry?

Let us begin by looking at the context of the passage cited at the top of this chapter. Jesus is discussing the cost of discipleship. In a burst of irrational enthusiasm, one said, "Lord, I will follow You wherever You go" (verse 57). Jesus let him know that he was in for a life of deprivation (verse 58). Another said, "Lord, let me first go and bury my father" (verse 59). Jesus let him know that there was no higher priority than to "go and preach the kingdom of God" (verse 60). As Warren Wiersbe has cogently remarked: "He was worried about someone else's funeral when he should have been planning his own" (The Bible Exposition Commentary, Volume I, Victor Books, A Division of Scripture Press Publications Inc., 1989, p. 209). Still another wanted to first go home and bid his loved ones goodbye (verse 61), leading Christ to say, "No one, having put his hand to the plow, and looking back, is fit for the kingdom of God" (verse 62). Burton Coffman has observed: "Jesus knew of the pressures the man would encounter at home and the persuasions that would thwart discipleship" (Commentary on the New Testament, the Gospel of Luke, StudyLight.org).

The man who preaches the gospel (or who plans to preach the gospel) must establish, develop, and maintain an ever-growing relationship with God. While all Christians are to be men and women of God, there is a special sense in which a preacher of the gospel is a man of God (cf. 1 Timothy 6:11; 2 Timothy 3:16-17). In His high priestly prayer, Jesus declared, "And this is eternal life, that they may know You, the only true God, and Jesus Christ whom You have sent" (John 17:3). While this applies to all who would gain eternal life, it is especially imperative that the preacher truly know God and His Son, Jesus Christ. If it is true that one cannot teach what he does not know, then it is true that a preacher cannot lead others to know God if he himself does not know God and is not constantly growing in his relationship with the Lord! The greatest of all preachers (other than Christ Himself) said, "But what things were gain to me, these I have counted loss for Christ. But indeed I also count all things loss for *the excellence of the knowledge of Christ Jesus my Lord,* for whom I have suffered the loss of all things, and count them as rubbish, that I may gain Christ and be found in Him, not having my own righteousness, which is from the law, but that which is through faith in Christ, the righteousness which is from God by faith, *that I may know Him and the power of His resurrection,* and the fellowship of His sufferings, being conformed to His death, if, by any means I may attain to the resurrection from the dead" (Philippians 3:7-11, emphasis mine, hf).

We do not need to be afraid to talk about knowing God and Christ. We are not talking about some fuzzy, highly emotional feeling–something better felt than told, something based on subjectivism rather than objective truth, as set forth in scripture. We are talking about coming to a knowledge of the one true God (Acts 17:22-28), to an understanding that Christ is the only way to the Father (John 14:6), to a realization of the necessity of dying to sin and being made alive to God by obedience to the gospel (Romans 6:1-14; Ephesians 2:1-10), and to the reality that we must "be steadfast, immovable, always abounding in the work of the Lord, knowing that [our] labor is not in vain in the Lord" (1 Corinthians 15:58). A gospel preacher must fight the good fight, finish the race, and keep the faith (2 Timothy 4:7). He must lay "aside every weight, and the sin which so easily ensnares us, and . . . run with endurance the race that is set before us, looking to Jesus, the author and finisher of our faith" (Hebrews 12:1-2). "For the eyes of the Lord run to and fro throughout the whole earth, to show Himself strong on behalf of those whose heart is loyal to Him" (2 Chronicles 16:9).

To be faithful over the long haul, the preacher must build on the rock (Matthew 7:24), which Rock is Christ (1 Corinthians 10:4). The preacher who is faithful over the long haul will be motivated by the two greatest commandments: unrestricted and unrestrained love for God and sincere love for one's fellowman equal to self-love (Matthew 22:37-39). A devoted preacher of the gospel will be constrained by the love of Christ (2 Corinthians 5:14), and all that he does will be done in love (1 Corinthians 16:14). Regardless of the heartaches, heartbreaks, set backs, disappointments, and discouragement that he faces, the man of God will say with another man of God, "But none of these things move me; nor do I count my life dear to myself, so that I may finish my race with joy, and the ministry which I have received from the Lord Jesus Christ, to testify to the gospel of the grace of God" (Acts 20:24).

How does the preacher (young or old) grow in his relationship with God so that, come what may, he is faithful over the long haul? Here are some practical suggestions that have been helpful to me during a ministry extending now over sixty years.

1. Study the Bible to know God, to know His will, to get to His great heart and mind. While it is important/essential for the preacher to study the Bible to prepare sermons and lessons, he also needs to read the Bible for his own spiritual growth and enrichment. It is not enough to know how to refute error, prove a point, or win a religious argument against false teachers. The preacher must also nourish his own soul on the word of God. "And now, brethren, I commend you to God

and to the word of His grace, which is able to build you up and give you an inheritance among all those who are sanctified" (Acts 20:32). While spoken to elders, these words are of equal force to preachers. "Man (and especially the man of God, hf) shall not live by bread alone, but by every word that proceeds from the mouth of God" (Matthew 4:4).

2. Engage in intimate, personalized prayer, rather than routine, ritualistic prayer. We need to be real and we need to be honest with God when we pray. We need to make time to sit down, think, and reflect on what we really need to talk with God about! An on-going prayer list is helpful. We would do well to make many of our prayers nothing other than prayers of thanksgiving, in which we ask for nothing but only thank the Lord for what we already have received. We might also try a lot more confession. Preachers also have sins to confess, repent of, and ask forgiveness for. We have weaknesses we need to acknowledge to the only One who can help us overcome them. Too, we might sometimes offer prayer in which our only purpose is to acknowledge the greatness of God and to praise Him for His greatness and power, His grace and mercy, His kindness and love.

When we really know someone, we are not afraid to open up with that person, bare our feelings, show our vulnerability, and talk about our hopes, our dreams, our aspirations, and our frustrations. Abraham is the only person in the Bible who is specifically called "the friend of God" (2 Chronicles 20:7; Isaiah 41:8; James 2:23). Abraham was not afraid to be direct in his appeal to God and to even try to bargain with God on behalf of Sodom (Genesis 18:23-33). The man of God today who truly knows God and is God's friend will have that same kind of intimate prayer life. I pray on my bed at night, while walking at the YMCA, while mowing my lawn, while driving my car, while sitting at my desk studying, while sitting in my reading chair, at meal time, with my wife, in the assembly with my brother and sisters, as well as at other times. Don't leave prayer out of your life; don't leave prayer behind! That is what the apostle meant when he said, "Pray without ceasing" (2 Thessalonians 5:17).

3. Fear God rather than man. This fear is not in the sense of being afraid of God, but in the sense of reverence, awe, and holy respect, recognizing that it is to God and not to any man that we are ultimately accountable. "And do not fear those who kill the body but cannot kill the soul. But rather fear Him who is able to destroy both soul and body in hell" (Matthew 10:28). Unfortunately, preachers are sometimes more concerned about what man thinks and says than they are with what God thinks and says. While we are to "love the brotherhood," we also are to "fear God" (I Peter 2:17). While we are to be governed by the truth, "If it be possible, as much as depends on you, live peaceably with all men" (Romans 12:18), this is not to be done at the expense of compromising the truth of

God's word. To maintain a strong relationship with God, a faithful preacher will not allow himself to be intimidated by peer pressure or by brotherhood cliques. Our first loyalty is to God!

4. Be humble and submissive. Don't think of self as king of the mountain, all-sufficient of oneself. It is easy, if one is not careful, to push God out to the circumference of our lives rather than making Him the center. Preachers are not exempt from this danger. Many years ago, a devout Christian in a public prayer in a worship assembly of God's people, said, "Lord, we are so stubborn and so slow to give ourselves up to You and Your way." Did he not speak the truth? Do we not all—preachers included—face this danger? And so once again we call attention to the counsel of the wise man: "Trust in the Lord with all your heart, and lean not on your own understanding; in all your ways acknowledge Him, and He shall direct (make smooth or straight, footnote) your paths. Do not be wise in your own eyes; fear the Lord and depart from evil. It will be health to your flesh, and strength to your bones" (Proverbs 3:5-8).

So, "before I go," I want to encourage all gospel preachers–young and old–to be faithful over the long haul by establishing and nurturing a strong, intimate relationship with God through the application of the biblical principles set forth in this chapter.

13

BEING A CHRISTIAN AT HOME

Larry Acuff

They see you every Sunday in the pulpit, they see you teaching a class, they see you entertaining the brethren either at a restaurant, at home or at a church function; but, is it the real you? While we are familiar with Bible passages such as, "For none of us liveth to himself, and no man dieth to himself" (Rom. 14:7), we may not always relate this to our relationships in our homes as gospel preachers.

Preachers with small children do not need a tape recorder; because those little ones will remember everything you say and do. They may not remember to say thank you when someone gives them a piece of candy but, they will remember very easily the wrong word you said at the dinner table or a slip of the tongue in a sermon. Impressionable children.

Most preachers are concerned about their families and have heard all the war stories of how a preacher neglected his family, and it created havoc in his life. Most preachers can relate the Biblical examples of Eli, Samuel and David (1 Sam. 3:13; 1 Sam. 13-16).

Having a family is a blessing to a preacher. Solomon wrote, "Whoso findeth a wife findeth a good thing, and obtaineth favour of the LORD" (Prov. 18:22). David gave us this great verse about children, "Lo, children are an heritage of the LORD: and the fruit of the womb is his reward. As arrows are in the hand of a mighty man; so are children of the youth. Happy is the man that hath his quiver full of them: they shall not be ashamed, but they shall speak with the enemies in the gate (Ps. 127:3-5).

A preacher must be a Christian in the home because his soul's salvation depends on it, as well as, that of his family. Nothing wrecks the cause of Christianity more than hypocrisy. Have you ever wondered why Christian young ladies do not want to marry preachers, or why young men are not encouraged to be preachers?

I know a lady who did not want to marry a preacher (Incidentally, however, she did). When questioning her as to the reason why she felt this way, it went back to her childhood days in the local congregation. She was friends with the preacher's daughter and often visited in their home; and it was what she saw in the home that helped determine her attitude. Members of a local congregation develop an attitude about their preacher based on his home life. It is essential that his home life portray the Christian life.

The same is true when it comes to young men desiring to preach. Perhaps young boys have had an association with the preacher's children (referred to as PKs) and made observations as a result of being in the home; so, it is essential that the preacher be a Christian in the home and not just in the pulpit.

The Talk

The most basic attribute that I wanted my children, the church and the community to see is the love that I have for my wife. I will never forget hearing Bro. Ira North, many years ago, say, "If Papa loves Mama and Mama loves Papa you don't have to worry about the children." This is true. If the evidence of love for the wife is seen in the home, the message that comes from the pulpit is going to be more powerful. This doesn't mean perfection on the part of the preacher but that the efforts are sincere.

One of the sad situations that occur in the preacher's family is that the wife sees herself as being in second place. I remember one occasion when I was determined to attend a lectureship, which happened to be several hundred miles away from where we lived, my wife did not want to me to go. I guess I thought she was selfish since our children were in school and she and they could not go. For whatever reason I was not attuned to her real feelings in the matter. I went to the lectureship; however, I found out later that she was afraid to be at home alone because our house had been broken into in recent months. That basic attribute of making sure that the wife does not feel that she is in second place in the life of her husband is necessary to be a Christian in the home.

Our wives love us, and they love the church. They, as we, want to put the church first; but at the same time there must be that balance. We as husbands must see that the wife does not feel that she is in competition with the Lord and His work.

The preacher's communication with his family is vital to being a Christian in the home. Does he express his love for his wife and children? " Let the words of my mouth, and the meditation of my heart, be acceptable in thy sight, O Lord, my strength, and my redeemer" (Ps. 19:14), also applies to the home. If he is hateful to his family and uses language that is not uplifting, it can overshadow a good sermon on Sunday. He should be very careful in his conversation with his wife or it can be very detrimental.

As a preacher, using the right words is important. It was always important to me for my children to see the affection, the love and appreciation I had for their mother. I never wanted any doubt in their minds about our relationship. Children learn from what they see.

In the Old Testament there was a man by the name of Nabal, and the Bible's description of him is; "Now the name of the man was Nabal, and the name of his wife Abigail. The woman was discerning and beautiful, but the man was harsh and badly behaved; he was a Calebite" (1 Sam. 25:3 ESV). What preacher would want to be described like that? How wonderful it is to see a preacher who is gentle to his wife and children– not harsh, not badly behaved. Being respectful with your language in communicating with your children is equally as essential. You may holler from the pulpit but watch the hollering at home. As a preacher, being a Christian in the home, means that I show respect to my children in my conversation with them. Calling my children "idiot" or "stupid" would not fit the profile that I wanted displayed in their life.

Teaching the love of Jesus is seen in the language you use before your children. We never used euphemism to emphasize a point. Such terminology as "darn" or "heck" or the most often used "OMG" were not uttered in our home. I was always taught that those who use the wrong kind of language were ignorant and knew nothing better to say.

I wanted my children to use the right words, and I wanted them to have respect for their mates when the time came for them to have their families, so it behooved me to display that kind of attitude, attribute and activity in our home.

The song, "Be careful little mouth what you speak, be careful little eyes what you see, be careful little ears what you hear; for the father up above is looking down in love..."

The Walk

Don't say one thing and do another. Being a Christian in the home is simply that. It was my goal to have my family see the spirit of Christ. How do you do that? The above words dealt with the communication in the home.

The second is by the way you live your life every day including your Bible study, prayer life, and the way you handle situations that arise. Your interaction with your wife, children, and neighbors all tell a story about your Christian life.

In our family, we spent a lot of time together. Meals were eaten together. For most of the schools days, we drove and picked up the children. We arose at four in the morning to take the children on their paper route and went with them to collect every Friday. We went to every ball game, band activity or whatever activity in which they were involved. The entire family went on the gospel meetings in which I preached, even taking them out of school on occasions. In the summer they attended every VBS in which I taught. On one occasion, I was teaching VBS in a neighboring congregation and the local preacher came to me and ask me to tell my son not to answer every question asked in his class. You see, that was the third or fourth VBS we had been to and, the congregations had been using the same material so he knew all the answers. We never failed to take a vacation with our children, but my wife and I also took a vacation every year without the children (they visited grandparents).

Being a Christian at home meant involving the entire family. In Hebrews when the Bible reveals, "By faith Noah, being warned of God of things not seen as yet, moved with fear, prepared an ark to the saving of his house; by the which he condemned the world, and became heir of the righteousness which is by faith" (Heb. 11:7). The scripture says, "Prepared an ark to the saving of his house." Noah saved his family. You don't save a family by being righteous in the pulpit and a scoundrel at home.

Here is a good phrase, "Practice what you preach." Practice it in your talk and in your walk. Several years ago, a gospel preacher by the name of Mid McKnight, wrote a book on the family entitled, Vestibules of Heaven. The premise of it is that the home was the Vestibule of Heaven. Being a Christian in the home makes us better preachers. Guard your life. Never counsel a lady in private where there would ever be suspicion about your actions. Respect your children, because they are an extension of you. One day my son came to me and said, "Dad, can I ask you to do something?"

Of course my reply was, "What?"

He said, "Would you please not volunteer me to do things without asking me first?"

It was not uncommon for me to say, "Oh, Jim will do that." I agreed with him.

Being a Christian in the home means doing what you say you will do so be careful about promises. If you promise to take the children somewhere–take them. If you promise to discipline them–discipline them. Make sure your word is good. Yes, situations arise beyond your control, but your family learns to respect you when you do what you say you

Preachers not only teach at the church building, but they also teach at home. Parents teach by their actions. Our daughter, while sitting in her mother's lap, made this comment, "Mommie, when I grow up to be a mommie, will you teach me to be a lady?" She may not have been sure of the order of things but she had the concept.

Being a Christian in the home means loving your wife and children and living in such a way that their lives are influenced by what they see. Using an Old Testament question that Isaiah asked Hezekiah, "What have they seen in your house?" (2 Sam. 20:15) This would be good for all of us to ask. What have our wives and children seen in our homes? I know some dedicated gospel preachers who have wonderful families. They are an inspiration to all. I preached a sermon entitled, "If My Children Were Three Again." We all wish for another opportunity, but there are no do-overs. Now I have grandchildren all of whom have been baptized into Christ. Can I stop being a Christian in the home? Absolutely not. Pa is still a preacher, and he is still in the home.

Be a Christian in the home.

14

TEACHING A CLASS

Gerald Romine

Jesus was the master teacher. Anyone desirous of teaching his word would do good to study his methods of teaching.

Acts 1:1 says, "he began both to do and teach." Before trying to teach, one should be a doer. Jesus has set the example for us.

I Peter 4:11: "If any man speak let him speak as the oracles of God, if any man minister let him do it of the ability God has given."

James 3:1, James says, "My brethren be not many teachers knowing ye shall receive the heavier judgment."

I do not believe James is discouraging teaching. He is emphasizing the importance of teaching the right thing. The religion of Christ (Christianity) is a teaching religion. Jesus' commission to the disciples was that they should teach the people, baptize the taught, and further teach them to observe all things commanded. Teaching is a privilege and an opportunity. Not everyone wants to be a teacher but we are commanded to teach. We have different areas in which we can teach.

One might not be able to teach a class but be excellent in a one-on-one situation. Whenever one teaches, he must be prepared. Being a teacher, you are directing the thoughts of the students at that moment. What you teach can have an important impact on the lives of those being taught. In fact, that is why we teach.

Not everyone is going to prepare the same way. Let us take a class situation. Usually Bible classes follow a set pattern. However, one could be assigned a subject to teach. In either situation, the teacher should be prepared. First of all, see what God's word has to say about the subject. We can always rely on God's word. As one studies a subject from time to time, in most cases, he will observe something new that he has not noticed in previous studies. See what God's word teaches and find scriptures that substantiate the teaching. Suppose the question is asked, and be sure to always welcome questions, is there just one church?

Ephesians 4 says that there is one body. It does not say what the body is but Ephesians 1:22, 23 tells us. This verse says the church is the body of Christ. I strongly encourage the asking of questions. We may not in every situation know the purpose or motive of the question. Jesus was asked a lot of questions. He knew the motive for each. He always paid attention to the question that was asked.

In preparing for a class, try to think of questions that might be asked. Be sure that you are prepared to answer the questions. There are situations when you simply will not know the answer. Admit that you do not know the answer but assure the student that you will do your best to find an answer. I was in an open forum at Freed-Hardeman several years ago. I do not remember the question nor the subject being discussed. However, I do remember Bro. Gus Nichols did not agree with the answer given. He informed the audience that he did not agree and that he was not prepared to defend his position at that time. He did assure everyone he would be prepared the next day.

The teacher has the responsibility of teaching, disciplining, and controlling the class. Do not let anyone take control of your class. It likely will not be in every class but sooner or later someone will try to take over the class. We have the responsibility of being respectful. We have the right to expect that of others but there are times when individuals will try you. Keep calm and control of the situation. As a teacher, you will face debatable questions. Debate is always good, but control the situation. Sum up a debatable question by giving what you believe the Bible teaches with regards to the question. There will be times when you are not sure of a correct answer. In such situations, express your opinion but emphasis that it is only an opinion.

Making sufficient preparation is very important. We cannot teach that we do not know. We will never know all there is to know about many Bible subjects. We should ever be trying to increase our knowledge of the Word of God. Study the material to be taught. Always let God's word guide us as we prepare a lesson. There are valuable helps available. When you have access to these helps, use them but keep in mind they are not inspired of God. God's word completely furnishes us unto every good work. We all at one time or another are like the Ethiopian eunuch. He was reading the scripture but admitted he did not understand what he was reading. Like him, we need someone to help us. That is our job as a teacher. If we can help someone to have a better understanding of God's word, we are doing our job. We should never feel that we know all there is to know. If we keep studying and teaching, we will become better at the job.

Teaching is a privilege but it does have its responsibilities. Let us be thankful for the privilege and accept the responsibility.

15

SPEAKING IN GOSPEL MEETINGS AND SPECIAL EVENTS

W.T. Allison

My Conversion and Life as a Christian

I was not reared in a Church of Christ home. My parents were Baptist (Freewill and Missionary Baptist). I was taught in Sunday school not to have anything to do with the Church of Christ and Catholics. This was my mindset for the first twenty-three years of my life. I met Shelby Jean Addison (a faithful member of the Church of Christ) and we were married on July 13, 1957. My wife and I fought a religious battle for four years. During this time, I read my Bible to prove my wife wrong. The more I read and studied I became more and more persuaded that New Testament Christianity was the direction my heart was leading me. On August 9, 1961, I was baptized into Christ. This was the single greatest decision in my life. I attribute my conversion to the faithfulness of my sweet wife who lived the Christian life before me.

I supported my family by working for Southern Natural Gas Company located in Birmingham, Alabama. Later, I worked for the 3M Company in Guin, Alabama. This plant manufactured reflective products. I had a great job with wonderful benefits and the promise of a secure future. Once I was converted, the making of reflective products didn't appeal to me anymore. I had a higher calling in a different direction. My heart was set on preaching the "good news" of Jesus Christ. I wanted God to use me and my talent in expanding the "kingdom of God." When I came up out of the watery grave of baptism, I automatically had a prospect list with the name of my mother and father at the top of the list. It took about six years through intense study to convert them to Christ.

Once they were converted, they became great soul-winners for Jesus as they attended the Hamilton Church of Christ in Hamilton, Alabama. Through the encouragement of Bro. M. C. Mills, an elder at Hamilton, I was given the opportunity to begin preaching. This journey took me over fifty two years in the service of the Lord. I preached for the Detroit Church of Christ (Detroit, Alabama), Hamilton Church of Christ (Hamilton, Alabama), Creekwood Church of

Christ (Mobile, Alabama), Guin Church of Christ (Guin, Alabama) and presently at the Sulligent Church of Christ (Sulligent, Alabama). I served as the President of the Board at Maywood Christian Camp for about 20 years.

During the fifty two years of preaching, I have served under the oversight of forty-four elders and never had a bad experience with any of those elders. They gave me the freedom to travel "as an evangelist" (2 Timothy 4:5).

In those fifty two years, God opened the door for me to preach in 800+ gospel meetings, lectureship and special events. If I could give an eldership any advice, it would be to give your preacher the help necessary to evangelize the world. As an evangelist, I conducted twenty overseas campaigns that resulted in many congregations being established. All of this is to the "glory of God and the up building of His Kingdom."

Philip Was My Example as an Evangelist

Paul and his company came to Caesarea to the house of Philip, the evangelist (Acts 21:8). Philip was one of the seven men selected to minister to the widows (Acts 6:5). He took the gospel to the city of Samaria which led to many converts. It was during this time that the angel of the Lord directed Philip to preach to the Ethiopian eunuch thus leading to his conversion (Acts 8:26-39) and the possible conversion of the nation of Ethiopia.

In studying the life of Philip, we are impressed with the fact that Philip was a SERVANT, a MISSIONARY and a PERSONAL EVANGELIST (in that order). There are ten spiritual qualities that every evangelist must have to be successful:

1. Philip was a righteous man or of honest report (Acts 6:3).

2. Philip was a compassionate man (Acts 6:1).

3. Philip was a man full of the Holy Ghost and wisdom (Acts 6:3).

4. Philip was a sensitive man (Acts 6:1).

5. Philip was a man of courage (Acts 8:1-5).

6. Philip was a man that made himself available to God (Acts 8:27).

7. Philip was a man that was tactful (Acts 8:30).

8. Philip was a man that was precise in his preaching (Acts 8:35).

9. Philip was a man that was decisive (Acts 8:37).

10. Philip was a man with initiative...he ran (Acts 8:30).

No person who is a Christian can leave out any of these qualities that are found in the life of Philip and be successful as an evangelist.

Are you a SERVANT of the Lord?

Do you have a MISSIONARY HEART for the lost of this world?

Are you a SOUL-WINNER for Jesus?

The missing piece of the evangelism puzzle is found in (Romans 9:1-3 and Romans 10:1). The missing piece is the "burden for souls." This seems to be lost among the 21st Century Christians. Where are the servants? Where is the heart for mission work? Where are the soul-winners in your congregation? Philip is my spiritual hero. I challenge everyone to emulate the life of Philip.

With all that I have written about Philip, one more thing should impress each of us about the life of Philip is that he had a real BURDEN for LOST MANKIND. Do I? Do you?

My Concern for the Church and the Next Generation

If our numbers of conversions decrease as much in the next twenty years as it has in the past twenty years, many congregations will cease to be. When I was converted to Christ, the Church of Christ was the fastest growing religious group in the U.S. We were growing at the rate of 125%. This was attributed to two things: (1) We were very conservative in our theology and (2) We placed great emphasis on personal evangelism. International Bible College (Heritage Christian University) would host an evangelism workshop and several thousand would attend. We were interested in saving the lost of our community.

I want to ask the younger generation this question: Are you interested in people?

We must realize that we are in the people business. I was at monthly preacher's meeting where a discussion was taking place about the work of a preacher. Some were lamenting the fact they didn't have time to study. There were members with problems that were taking up much of their time. They asked me for my opinion. I told them as far as I could glean from my study of the Bible, the preacher was in the PEOPLE business. PEOPLE are our #1 business. When we get rid of the PEOPLE, we are out of business.

Preachers are the most visible representative of the local church. You need to be seen out in town, hospital, nursing homes, postal office, funerals and anywhere hurting people are found. When some tragedy happens, you need to be among the first there. Prejudice is placed aside when a person is hurting. It's the preachers opportunity so serve others.

What Is the Future of Gospel Meetings and Special Events?

Have gospel meetings lost their effectiveness? The month long meetings are a thing of the past. We have gone from three week meeting down to three day meeting down to a one day meeting...and still we can't get our members to faithfully attend this meeting. No, gospel meeting have not lost their effectiveness. The problem is not with the gospel meeting. The problem is with the church.

A GOSPEL MEETING needs to be turned into a REVIVAL. Revival is the restoration of life to something that is dead or unconscious. A revival is where the Word of God is taught, worship to God in spirit and truth is rendered, Jesus Christ is exalted, lost souls are led to Christ, the membership is edified/encouraged, and a spiritual feast is enjoyed by all.

There is no way to reach the lost in a revival if the lost are not present. The membership cannot be revived if they are too busy to attend. To have a successful revival, every member must prepare his own heart for the meeting. Each member must invite others to the revival. Every member needs to try to restore the unfaithful.

Every member needs to pray for the success of the revival. Every member needs to attend every service of the meeting. Who has the responsibility to "light the fires" for a revival in the local church? The elders and preacher are faced with this task. It takes more than printing a brochure and sending it to the local congregations to attend. It takes the local membership to pray, promote and personally invite the lost to attend.

There are three major keys to a successful revival:

APPEAL to God (prayer)

ADVERTISE (talk about it for weeks...promote it until the membership is tired of hearing you talk about it) and

ATTEND every service of the revival yourself.

Seven steps to an effective revival:

(1) REALIZE the need,

(2) PRIORITIZE your time,

(3) AGONIZE over the lost,

(4) ORGANIZE for the revival,

(5) PUBLICIZE by using every means of advertising,

(6) EVANGELIZE by getting personally involved, and

(7) MAXIMIZE the importance of the revival. "Seek first the Kingdom of God."

In closing, I want each of us to never lose faith in the power of the SEED (word of God) nor in the SOIL (heart of the sinner).

"Be not weary in well doing: for in due season we shall reap, if we faint not." It takes PEOPLE to win PEOPLE "to Christ."

Remember, we are in the PEOPLE BUSINESS. That should be the #1 priority in the life of younger men in the ministry and I wanted to convey this to you BEFORE I GO.

16

TRAINING YOUR FAMILY FOR MINISTRY

Jim Faughn

First, I hope you will allow me to say that I am, at once, honored, humbled, and confused about being asked to participate in this project. I am honored because of the high regard I have for those who are spearheading this effort. I am humbled by the fact that they might think I have something worthwhile to offer. I am also confused because I am both far too young and far too inexperienced to participate!

The information I received was directed to brethren who were at least seventy years old and who had been preaching for at least forty years. Since I am a mere child of sixty-six and have been preaching for only about thirty-six of those years, I am not too sure how much I can contribute. I will do my best to not allow my youth and inexperience to detract from what I write.

My age and my "years of service" as a full-time preacher may not be the only ways in which I am different from some of the other contributors to this project. Some of my background may also be somewhat different.

Since I did not begin to preach "full-time" until I was thirty years of age, I got a later start than many preachers. I am quite sure that our children were far too young to remember when I was not a preacher. Our daughter was four years old and our son was nine months old when I began preaching.

Even though they do not remember those days when I was not preaching, they have heard stories and talked with people who knew their mother and me during those early years of our marriage. They know that both parents were school teachers back in those days. They know that their mother put that career "on hold" for several years in order to be at home with them. They know that their father was baptized into Christ after he married their mother.

Maybe the most important thing they have learned from those stories is that their parents were involved in the work of a local congregation before their father ever began preaching. It is my prayer that, because of our earlier years and what our children know about them, they grew up with the idea that this thing called "ministry" is not only for the "trained professionals." A couple of school teachers, one of whom had been fairly recently converted, could actually contribute something to the work of the Lord.

I am a firm believer in the idea that much of what children learn is caught rather than (or at least along with) taught. Since that is what I believe to be true, it is also my prayer that my children "caught" the idea that I viewed my role as a full-time preacher as only one form of ministry.

I have tried my best during my years as a preacher to teach by both word and deed that the only difference between any other Christian and me is in terms of function. In the words the Holy Spirit used to inspire Paul, "there are varieties of service, but the same Lord; and there are varieties of activities, but it is the same God who empowers them all in everyone" (1 Cor. 12:5-6, ESV).

I am especially intrigued by how the same author and the same penman presents this concept in another passage:

"For by the grace given to me I say to everyone among you not to think of himself more highly than he ought to think, but to think with sober judgment, each according to the measure of faith that God has assigned. For as in one body we have many members, and the members do not all have the same function, so we, though many are one body in Christ, and individually members one of another" (Rom. 12:3-5, ESV).

Accordingly, there are some things I pray that my children caught when they were growing up in the home of a gospel preacher. Among those things would be the following:

• They had a father who resisted being called brother Faughn—unless everybody in a particular situation was being addressed as brother or sister. Hopefully, my children remember a home in which their father tried to not set himself apart from, or consider himself to be aloof from, any other faithful Christian.

• Along the same lines, my children grew up in a home where the father did not consider himself to be the minister for the congregations where he preached, but a minister.

• Ministry was not about schedules and programs. It was about a lifestyle. The congregations in which my children grew up did, indeed, have various service projects, programs, etc. Hopefully, though, they caught the idea that ministry was not limited to these activities.

• One does not have to be some sort of super Christian in order to minister. My children saw very early on, and on a very regular basis, the fact that their father was not, by any stretch of the imagination, perfect. They saw (and still see) the real me. They knew better than anybody else, other than their mother, if the guy in the pulpit was genuine or not. They may have (hopefully) picked up on the idea that a person does not have to be perfect in order to be a minister. They heard people refer to their dad as a minister and they knew that he certainly was not perfect. They saw him at his worst. Maybe they developed the idea that, if God can use somebody like their dad, He can use anybody. I have read somewhere that God only uses imperfect people to accomplish His mission because imperfect people are all He has at his disposal. My children saw that up close and personal.

• It helps to involve all of the members of the family as much as possible. While there may be (and are) some places and activities that are not child friendly, many ways can be found in which every member of the family can be involved in some form of ministry to others. It seems to me that this could and should begin at home. Children should be taught that they are "not to be served, but to serve." If those words sound somewhat familiar, they are from the lips of our Savior and are recorded in Matthew 20:28 as translated in the English Standard Version. It may be remembered that the King James Version uses the words "ministered unto" and "minister" in this verse. If the concept of service (ministry) begins at home, it has a good chance of branching out to other places.

It may be at this point that the reader is thinking, Why has this been all about what your children may have learned from you. Didn't your wife have any role at all in their training?

It would be the height of absurdity for me to claim that whatever training our children received during their formative years came solely from me. I do not know who came up with the idea that "behind every good man there is a good woman," but I believe it is much more accurate to say, "beside every good man there is a good woman." At least that's how I view it in our family.

I would affirm that the training our children got concerning ministry came from their mother more than from their father. For example they learned (and had modeled) before them some very important things. What they saw was that ministry is about...

• Teamwork. Our children were fortunate enough to see a mother who was not pulling in a different direction from the path their father was on. They saw that ministry was/is about working together in a physical family and in the Lord's family. As I type these words, I am thinking of a telephone conversation I had just last evening. One of the members where I preach was talking to me about my wife and me. In particular, she was commenting on how effective she thinks we are as a team. I appreciated her assessment. I also am very aware of who the MVP of the team is --- and it isn't me.

• Sacrifice. A career was sacrificed. Time was sacrificed. Effort was sacrificed. All of this (and more) was done so that their mother could minister as a wife, a mother, a daughter to her older parents, a daughter-in-law to her husband's parents, a contributing member of the local congregation, and, basically, to anybody who needed her.

• Agape love. Our children did not just hear from their father and from others about this wonderful type of love written about in their New Testaments. They saw it lived out day in and day out by their mother.

• Humility. I'm sure that our children observed the times when somebody bragged on their dad for a sermon he had preached, a class he had taught, or some other time when he had been in the limelight. I'm sure that they also observed that, it was during those times when they would see their mother either standing beside him or maybe off some distance away just smiling and allowing him to bask in the glow. It was also during those times that they probably thought: We know the truth. We know how valuable mom is to this family and to this congregation. We also know that she doesn't mind being in the shadows.

• Respect. Yes, my wife demanded that our children respect her–and me. Indeed, they learned that people in authority needed to be respected. All of that grew out of her deep respect for, and devotion to, God and His Word. It is my observation that this has carried over into their lives.

Both our son and our son-in-law are gospel preachers, but they are far from being the only ministers in our family. Their spouses also serve in so many ways. While, at this point, only one of our five grandchildren has been baptized into Christ, all of them are already learning the value of ministering to others. Their parents have found and developed some very unique ways to train them to think about and serve others.

For that reason, and because of my understanding of what ministry is really all about, I am blessed beyond measure to be able to say that we have a total of eleven ministers in our family.

In my opinion, it cannot get much better than that.

17

AN INTERVIEW WITH GEORGE BAILEY

The Jenkins Institute and George Bailey

George Bailey is not a great preacher just because he quotes a lot of Scriptures in his sermons (although he does that). Brother Bailey is not a great preacher just because he has a commanding voice (his voice is still powerful in his 90's). He is not a great preacher just because he knows how to turn a phrase, although he can do that as well as any man alive. He is not a great preacher just because of his amazing command of the English language (even though that is true). He is a great preacher because he loves the Lord, His Word, and the Church. To be in his presence is to see what a true Christian gentleman should be. He is kind, considerate, and caring. He loves life and he loves people.

Brother Bailey is the consummate preacher. There is perhaps no man among us who has done as much preaching as brother Bailey. He has literally preached around the world. He has often been called the Prince of Preachers. He is a unique preacher and chances of having another one just like him come along seem to be slim.

He is the true definition of the preacher's preacher.

Some time back we asked brother Bailey if we could interview him about preachers and preaching. When we first asked brother Bailey to participate in this project he seemed reticent to do so. He wasn't sure he had anything worth sharing (Oh, for more Preachers in the church like him who understand humility and service. We have way too many preachers who think that every thought they have needs to be put on display!)

One of the most outstanding characteristics of this man of God is his humility. If any preacher in our day has a right to be proud, George Bailey would be that man. Honestly, we doubt he realizes his greatness and the immeasurable good he has done for the church during his more than seventy-five years of preaching!

It was such a blessing to sit and listen to him as he answered the questions we had chosen. He would often give an answer and then he would say, "What are your thoughts about that?" Some of his answers came quickly, others required a little more thought. A couple of times he said, "Can we come back to that?"

Once or twice we would lose our train of thought and we would have to try to remember the question. A few times brother Bailey repeated himself, which was perfectly fine with us. The stories of his life are so engaging you could sit for hours and listen to the same stories over and over again.

Thanks to the marvel of modern technology we were able to record the interview on my iPhone. We have done our best to transcribe the answers from brother Bailey exactly as he gave them, with very little commentary. With these preliminary notes in mind, let's get to the good stuff.

TJI: Who influenced you most to become a preacher?

BROTHER BAILEY: G. A. Dunn, Gus Dunn. He knew that Bible almost by heart. He was an old time preacher. He'd get into an argument with himself, while he was preaching. He'd say, "Now brother Dunn, why did you say that?" Then he'd answer himself. I really learned a lot under his tutoring. I had a great respect for him.

And of course, N.B. Hardeman. (Then he said, "You took classes under him, didn't you?!!!!") He was not a scholar, but he gave us great information. And of course, my parents influenced me.

I can't remember a time when I didn't want to preach. I'd get syrup buckets and turn them over like they were seats, I preached to the cows, pigs, and chickens. Never converted a one of them, not one. I preached my first official sermon when I was fourteen in Kaufman, TX. I went to Freed Hardeman and met Ela Beth while we were there.

TJI: Where did you begin your work as a preacher?

BROTHER BAILEY: My first full-time preaching was in Weatherford, Oklahoma. They let me take some more classes while I was there. I was making $20.00 a week. I told the elders, this may be out of place, but would it be asking too much for you to give me a raise? They said, "how much George?" I said how about $5.00, they said, "how about $2.50?" I said, "Ela Beth is worth every bit of that!" They were fine men.

TJI: How long were your sermons when you first started preaching?

BROTHER BAILEY: I'd say about thirty minutes. I didn't always hold it to that, but I tried. I think everybody wanted me to cut them shorter.

TJI: What about other places you preached?

BROTHER BAILEY: We were first in Weatherford; there was Corsicana, then Oklahoma City, then Abilene, and then Dallas.

TJI: Brother Bailey, tell us about your preparation for preaching?

BROTHER BAILEY: I would research and gather as much material as I could find. Then I'd try to whittle it down so as not to make the sermons to long. I would spend time praying about it and studying that material.

TJI: You have a lot of sayings that some people call Bailyisms. Could you tell us how those came to be and give us a few of them?

BROTHER BAILEY: Some of them came natural to me. I like to play on words so that's how some of them came to me. I got to where I used it a lot. One of my favorites is, "If you don't work hard when you don't have to you'll have to work hard when you don't want to!" Another one is, "When a man thinks he's through learning, he is through!" Others are, "If we would keep the unity of the Spirit, then we must keep the spirit of unity!" "Jesus wants to be Lord in every man's life, but waits until each man makes Him Lord of his life."

TJI: If you could give some advice to young preachers what would you say to them?

BROTHER BAILEY: I'd say boys, "Study, study, study, study." You can't study too much. I really love to study. Sometimes you have to leave your office to be able to study. Everybody will want to come by and visit. There's nothing wrong with that but it can distract you from doing the important work of study.

I'd tell them to work hard to get along with their elders. I saw a sign in a Drs. Office that said, the success of this visit depends on which one of us is the Dr. I tried to never put myself in the place of telling the elders what to do. Let them decide. You can encourage them and you can make suggestions because there are times that preachers have taken over and tried to rule.

I would encourage young preachers to get to know and ask questions from the older preachers. Those relationships can be powerful. I wrote and talked to several preachers through the years and it was very helpful.

TJI: What do you believe to be the most important work of the preacher?

BROTHER BAILEY: Of course, as I mentioned study is so important. Nothing can take the place of study. I have always thought that visiting the hospitals was an important part of our work. I made that a practice and I believe it paid off. Hulen Jackson said to me one time, "People can forgive a preacher for a lot of things, but they will have difficulty forgiving him for not being there when they need him."

It is important to get to know the people in the church. And they will get to know you better also. Then when I was in meetings I'd choose one night and try to meet with all of the young men in the church who had preached or who would like to preach. I tried to encourage them in every way possible.

TJI: How important is it for the preacher to take time for his family?

BROTHER BAILEY: Oh, that's very important. I think a lot of preachers have missed the mark there; they didn't spend enough time with their family. I tried to spend time with both of my sons and took them on preaching trips with me. That is time that will never be regretted.

TJI: Do you have any thoughts about preachers having friends?

BROTHER BAILEY: Well, I think it will be natural that you have some close friends. It's okay to have a very best friend. It's good to have friends in the church and it's good to have friends who are preachers. I think it's important that you have one preacher that you are very close to as you do your work.

JTI: Should preachers take time off from work?

BROTHER BAILEY: I really do. I didn't do that as much as I think it should be done. I would recommend it highly. Some of our men have burned out rather quickly and taking time off might have prevented some of that. Some don't stop long enough to see what damage is being done. Getting rest will pay dividends.

TJI: Would you discuss the importance of preaching from the Scriptures?

BROTHER BAILEY: It is vitally important. You can't do what the Lord said, or be what the Lord said you should be if you don't preach from the Scriptures. It takes work and effort to memorize and preach from the Scriptures but it pays great dividends.

TJI: Would you mention something about the preacher's prayer life?

BROTHER BAILEY: It is very, very important. I can't say enough about it. I've often said you ought to pray as much as anything else. You have to spend a lot of time in prayer. Prayer is one of those things that will mark our life and who we are as preachers. Your life should be a constant prayer.

TJI: What do you think that preachers struggle with the most?

BROTHER BAILEY: One thing is pride. I think it is one of the most repulsive things in the world for a young preacher or an older one to think he is it. I used to talk to older preachers to find out how they dealt with pride and other problems.

TJI: What can preachers do to keep from developing too much pride?

BROTHER BAILEY: Give himself a slap. Pray about it. Work not to be arrogant. It is through pride that the Devil became the Devil. When somebody starts telling you how good you are, don't always believe it. Listen to others. I have been helped by so many others.

TJI: Are there any other words of advice you would want to give?

BROTHER BAILEY: I've been asked that question many times. I would say you need to budget your time. Everybody has the same number of hours from the most important person to the lowest. It's what you do with those hours in the week that count.

Spend a lot of time studying, a lot of time praying. You can't study and pray too much. Get to know the members of the church and those in the community who are not members. Spend time with as many as possible. We can learn so much from one another.

TJI: Thank you very much for taking this time with us. All of the preachers who read it will be very thankful. And thank you for the life you have lived before us.

BROTHER BAILEY: You are welcome and thank you. This has been a wonderful morning. May God bless all of the preachers who are doing their very best to serve Him. Let's pray together.

Made in the USA
Middletown, DE
20 July 2020

13182663R00106